A HUNDRED MILES AS THE CROW FLIES

by

RALPH CHURCHES

ISBN 0 646 39117 8

CENTRAL CHANCERY OF THE ORDERS OF KNIGHTHOOD
ST JAMES'S PALACE, SW1A 1BG
TELEPHONE - 01-834 2837 8 2838

21st June, 1945

The King has been graciously pleased to approve the award of the British Empire Medal (Military Division), in recognition of gallant and distinguished services in the field, to the undermentioned:-

No SX 5286 Private Ralph Frederick Churches, Australian Military Forces.

DEDICATION

To the valiant Slovene Partisans who, beyond the call of duty, risked so much to guide me and ninety eight other escaping prisoners-of-war across "a hundred miles as the crow flies" of enemy occupied country in August-September 1944 and no less to Ronte who so warmly welcomed me home and, over the intervening fifty years, has "minded" me with loving efficiency.

ACKNOWLEDGEMENT

I must acknowledge the efforts of my son, Neil Churches who has managed to convert my ill-typed manuscript to the form in which you are now reading it. I believe it was done with computers, an area of technology that has left me far behind. However it was done I am grateful to him for having acquired the know-how to do it as well as for his so generously sparing the necessary time.

CONTENTS

DEDICATION

ACKNOWLEDGEMENT

PREFACE

END NOTES

The Author

Ralph Churches was born in 1917, the eighth and youngest child of a pioneer farming family in the Murray Mallee of South Australia and learned early in life what it was to be a "battler". He took his primary education at various small one teacher schools and was sufficiently bright to win one of ten government scholarships for rural children which enabled him to go to the city and attend Adelaide High School where four years later he matriculated. It was 1934; the Great Depression was at its deepest; with his parents and three older brothers back home on the farm, there was no real place for him there, even if he had wanted it. He had seen enough of the thankless unremitting toil of pioneering farm life and returned to Adelaide to look for office work.

He maintained himself for eight months canvassing shoe repairs on commission until he managed to secure a position for himself with the State Bank of South Australia. After training in Head Office, he was posted, firstly to Renmark and subsequently to Wudinna in the west of the state. It was from here in June 1940 that he enlisted in the second A.I.F. in the process marrying Ronte on a ten day license.

He was posted to the 2/48 Batallion and sailed with that unit on the "Stratheden" on 17th November for the Middle East and disembarked just one month later at El Kantara, Egypt after a brief stopover in Colombo. He was posted to Corps Headquarters on allegedly "temporary secondment" in late January and participated in the first "Benghazi Derby". In March, still with the same formation, he was sent to Greece, where after advancing and retreating over almost the whole length of that country, he was captured by the Germans on the 6th May while trying, with three companions, to sail a dinghy to Crete.

On his return to Australia in November 1944 he was given three months leave and then posted to a prisoner-of-war camp at Murchison in Victoria as an interpreter. He was promoted sergeant and eventually discharged in November 1945.

He resumed work with the Bank but, after fifteen months, decided that he should try something more rewarding than the Bank's six pounds ten shillings a week. The Prudential Assurance Company granted him a franchise based on the township of Maitland where he was then resident. He was an instant success ranking among the Company's top salesmen when, ten years on, he accepted an offer from Legal and General Assurance to open a branch for them in Adelaide. In 1961 he transferred to Sydney as Manager, New South Wales.

He returned to Adelaide on retirement in 1979 where, with Ronte still by his side, he is active in his Probus Club, the Ex-Prisoners-of-War Association and, not least, his church where he is still a choir member. He and Ronte are the proud parents of a daughter, Bev and sons, Steven and Neil.

PREFACE

This is a true story - a story of an escape from a German Prisoner-of-War camp in August 1944. It tells of what is probably the largest successful break-out by British P.O.W. in World War II. No detailed account of it has ever previously been written so far as I know. TV Channel SBS 0/28 made an hour long feature film about it in 1985 which consisted, in the main, of reminiscences by ageing Slovene ex-Partisans and my English co-conspirator, Les Laws with some laudatory comments from me concerning the former.

A month or two prior to going to Slovenia to assist in making this film I had given a reporter from the Adelaide "Advertiser" an hour long interview on the subject mainly because I was disgusted with the widespread media coverage given to the so obviously bogus story of an Englishman who claimed to have been planted on *Abwehr*, the German Counter Intelligence agency before the war and to have served out the conflict communicating secret German information back to London. My story was given front page headlines by the "Advertiser" next day and was taken up by the press interstate but, like so much of the reporting in our daily papers, sub-editors had been at work on it and given more emphasis to some remarks I had made to the reporter outside the area of the principal subject concerning the wretchedness of the German P.O.W. cages in Greece and the horrors of the four day rail journey in over-crowded cattle trucks to Maribor a few kilometres south of the Austrian border with Slovenia over three years previous to the escape.

It might well asked why bother, after fifty one years, writing about a minor incident in a remote side-show of World War II and I would have to accept the question as a fair one to which there are a number of answers. Firstly, my own family together with a sizeable company of nieces nephews and their collective offspring have been pressing me for long years to get on with it. Secondly, I have never ceased to be conscious of the debt I will always owe those sturdy and resourceful guerillas, the Slovene Partisans who suffered unbelievable hardships and accepted such grievous casualties in defying the might of the Nazis and harassing their lines of communication. It seems to me that the Great Allies of World War II have never, then nor since, really acknowledged the extent to which those hardy freedom fighters contributed to Germany's final defeat, nor the price they paid in so doing. May this short account of my association with them, in however small a way, salute their valour.

As to the long delay, I, and everyone else who took part in the escape were categorically forbidden from either talking or writing about it. None of us had, to the best of my knowledge, been formally released from that ban. But when TV Channel SBS 0/28 contacted me in 1984 seeking my co-operation in making a film in Slovenia on the subject they assured me that it had been cleared with all authorities concerned. It was then, having retired from work some five years previously, that I decided to start some research to ensure that whatever I might write would be in line with the official record and, to that end, I opened up a correspondence with the Army Records Office which, after much to-ing and fro-ing obtained for me from Britain the debriefing statements taken from every member of the escape party in Foggia, Italy in September 1944.

These consisted entirely of routine answers to routine questions as to how we had been treated, what camps we had been in and such like. Each one was almost a carbon copy of the other. Significantly, there was no mention of the report covering the special debriefing of Les Laws and myself together or my second debriefing the following day.

Here I must go back fifty years or so: A bit over a month after arriving home I was recalled from leave and put on the Melbourne express, met at the Spencer Street Station by an Army officer with a staff car and taken to the military headquarters on St.Kilda Road. There I was most cordially received by a number of high ranking officers with red tabs on the collars of their tunics. I was gently but searchingly interrogated for several hours over a period of two days. To confirm my story they called in "Jimmy" Woods, one of the Melbourne members of our party.

To this day no record of that debriefing has been forthcoming. In fact I have just finished going through some of this correspondence and re-established that our Australian military records would appear to contain no reference to the escape other than the information supplied from the British sources mentioned above. They probably contain a copy of the citation attaching to the British Empire Medal I was awarded for my part in the operation. The people at the Australian War Memorial in Canberra were more interested and helpful; it was they who supplied me with a copy of the report submitted by Captain W.J.Hesslop N.Z.E.F. on the strength of which I received my BEM. It was they too who supplied me with the copy of an extract from the New Zealand War diary purporting to relate to the affair. The only details in that paper which were correct were the names of the New Zealanders involved. According to it the raid on the railway line at Ozhbalt was led by two British officers!

Les Laws was awarded a Distinguished Conduct Medal for his role in the affair. It seems incredible to me that an operation in respect of which two decorations "for gallant and distinguished services in the field" were awarded, one to an Australian - the same operation that liberated twelve Australian servicemen, does not receive at least, passing mention in the Australian War Diary.

I re-visited Slovenia with my wife in 1972 where we were feted up and down the length of the country for five days. The surviving veterans of the *Latsko Odred* from their Colonel down entertained us right royally. Franchek, by then Franjo Vesenjak, a Justice of the Supreme Court of Slovenia and Sveik, now France Gruden, gentleman farmer, particularly, greeted me literally with hugs and kisses; no long lost brother could have been more warmly welcomed. We made a passing visit again in 1977 by which time Cholo, otherwise Karel Cholnik had retired to his native Maribor after almost thirty years in Melbourne Australia where he had built up a large and successful business as a nurseryman. Our third visit was in 1985 in connection with the making of the telefilm, "March to Freedom" noted above. Naturally, on all three visits, our march across the country from north to south was discussed and re-hashed almost ad nauseam. I have revisited in daylight the farmhouse near which we were ambushed, I have seen again the spot where we crossed the Sava, I have been back to Semich and driven out the five or six kilometres to the area that served as the airstrip from which we were lifted in 1944, and, seeing it in the cold light of day, I must say that I understand why the young Flight Sergeant called our take-off a "dicey do" - tall trees lining a river at one end with sharply rising ground at the other not much more than a thousand metres distant seemed to me to be barely enough distance in which to get a laden DC3 airborne.

Having done all this, I am as confident as one can be after fifty years that this account of my escape and my journey home is accurate, at least as to broad detail. Where I have recorded direct speech, the words written may not be exactly those spoken - soldiers' vernacular, even today, may not be acceptable to some readers but I have tried to convey the substance of what was said.

It should be noted that the Slovene language, though using the Roman alphabet, has some differences in pronunciation. Thus "c" is pronounced "ts", so "Latsko" is written "Lacko". "C" with an inverted circumflex over it is pronounced English "ch". Thus "Cholnik" is written "Colnik" and "Semich" is written "Semic". "S" and "z" are also subject to modification; "s" with an inverted circumflex over it becomes English "sh" and "zh" the French "je". Thus "Shentilj" is written "Sentilj" and "Ozhbalt" "Ozbalt". For easier reading I have used English phonetics.

Now that is about enough for a preface; it's about time that you, the limited readership for which this tale is written, got on with reading it. As Shakespeare wrote in the prologue to his "Henry V", "Piece out our imperfections with your thoughts". I should also remind you that, in the same play, he had the hero King remark specifically of war veterans, "Old men forget and all shall be forgot, but they'll remember with advantages what feats they did that day."

So, with these admonitions from the bard, go to it. I hope you find the reading worth your time.

R.F.C.
Adelaide, July 1995.

CHAPTER ONE
SETTING THE SCENE

The following news item appeared in the Adelaide "News" on the ninth of October 1944.

S.A. SOLDIER ESCAPES FROM PRISON CAMP

Mrs. R. F. Churches, of Aroona road, Kilkenny, has received news that her husband, Private Churches, has escaped from a prisoner of war camp in Austria, and is safely behind Allied lines.

The first advice Mrs. Churches had was a cable from her husband, saying that he had escaped and was safe and well.

Military Records Office confirmed the news.

Another cable came from Cairo, with a message through the Red Cross to say he was well.

On Saturday she received an airgraph letter from him dated September 18, saying that he was safe with a New Zealand base unit, and hoped to be on his way to Australia shortly.

Private Churches was employed in the State Bank at Wudinna at the time of his enlistment in June, 1940. He was captured in Greece in May, 1941.

Private Churches

This is the story behind that brief report:

I was captured by the Germans at Cape Maleas in Greece on May 6 1941 and following the usual early vicissitudes of P.O.W. life found myself in a working camp in Southern Austria.

As various books, movies and TV programmes have been written around and about officer P.O.W. and the camps in which they were confined by the Germans it is necessary to understand at the outset the difference in the accommodation accorded to other ranks.

Under the Geneva Convention covering the treatment of P.O.W., officers could not be compelled to work for the detaining power and with the rarest of rare exceptions did not do so. N.C.O.'s could be forced to supervise prisoners at work, and other ranks could be forced to work. This being so, officers were confined under very tight security in large establishments known as *Oflags* (*Offizierlager*) usually for the duration. Except for the fact that their quarters were usually wooden barracks and that the prison "walls" consisted of 12 foot high double barbed wire fences well covered by searchlights and machine gun armed elevated sentry boxes, their situation was no different from that of any convict except that no labour could be enforced on them.

N.C.O.'s and other ranks, on the other hand, were invariably set to work by the zealous and optimistic Germans. Firstly they were registered in a *Stalag* (*Stammlager*) or main camp. This was also a large establishment of high security. It contained the administrative offices, both German and British, for all the prisoners registered as belonging to it: medical services, hospital, Red Cross, postal service, etc. From the *Stalag*, prisoners were let out to such employers as sought to hire them. The employer bore the cost of setting up a camp for his P.O.W. workers secured to the satisfaction of the military authorities and of providing suitable accommodation for such military guard as the *Wehrmacht* deemed necessary. These working camps or *Arbeitskommando* were scattered over the area administered by the *Stalag* wherever the work happened to be and might be anything up to 50 or 60 miles distant from it.

The significant difference between *Arbeitskommando* and *Stalag* was that the working camps themselves were not usually as well secured physically as the major establishments. Usually, there was only a single barbed wire fence, and the size of the place did not warrant elevated sentry boxes, searchlights and machine guns. Guards were usually in the ratio of one to ten prisoners and the armament was usually restricted to World War I repeating rifles. Other factors rendered rigid physical security less necessary. "British" other ranks in World War II with the exception of Australians were almost all conscripts; as prisoners they usually worked hard physically though rarely effectively six days a week and however keen they may have been to get home they tended as the months and years went by to accept the safety and comparative comfort of their present condition in preference to the rigours and hazards of active service of which they had already had such a distasteful sample.

From almost the moment of my capture, as a brash 23 year old, I was seized by a pride dictated conviction that somehow, some day, I would escape, and to this end set about learning the German language even during the first days. On arriving at my first *Arbeitskommando* via *Stalag XVIIIC* Maribor just on the Jugoslav side of the Austrian border, I saw that, for the potential escaper, the smaller establishment had far and away better possibilities.

From August 1941 I found myself during the following six months in a variety of working camps in Southern Austria from two of which I went A.W.L. I use the term A.W.L. advisedly as neither of these efforts, for lack of sustained and detailed planning warranted the description of "escape".

They could, however, be regarded as reconnaissances. Firstly they proved that there was no great effort either mental or physical involved in a temporary escape from custody and secondly I was able to find out something of what was needed in the way of knowledge and equipment before a complete and successful getaway could be undertaken with any degree of confidence.

However, two "escapes" the first of which netted me three days and the second seven days "bread and water" in the clink at *Stalag* had closed this particular avenue for the acquisition of knowledge. The next abortive attempt would undoubtedly see me transferred to a much less pleasant environment where a much higher degree of security would prevail.

By now it was April 1942 and I found myself in a camp of some 100 mixed Britishers (Tommies, Australians and New Zealanders) working on the reconstruction of a highway just on the Jugoslav side of the Austrian border some seven miles north of Maribor. What knowledge and equipment had I acquired for the main purpose? For a successful clean getaway, the first thing the escaper has to decide is his geographical objective. As *der Fuehrer* and his junior partner, *Il Duce* had everything in Europe with the exception of Sweden, Switzerland, Spain, Portugal and Turkey well under military control, this rather restricted the choice. Switzerland was 250 miles and Turkey 600 miles away, both distances "as the crow flies" and except as regards the nickname by which I was commonly known, I was not a crow[1]. Firstly I had no map but my memory of leaving standard geography as taught at Adelaide High School suggested that I would need to be a professional mountaineer to reach Switzerland by any route other than the heavily patrolled roads and an Olympic swimmer to reach Turkey without using the well guarded bridges over the many quite major rivers that lay between me and that country.

I therefore decided to follow Mr. Micawber's philosophy and "wait for something to turn up."

In the meantime I was, by virtue of my growing command of German, appointed camp interpreter which absolved me from physical toil on the end of pick, shovel and wheelbarrow. (The refinements of road construction by way of bulldozers, front end loaders and tip trucks had not yet reached the delightful hills and valleys of Styria)[2]. This circumstance left me with more free time to study German by talking to the guards, the civilian foremen on the job and the civilian tradesmen who supplied the camp.

It also automatically put me in charge of the twice weekly party which marched with a hand cart, under guard to the local village Shentilj (St. Egydi), to draw our rations and buy such uncontrolled merchandise as was available.[3] This also applied to the Sunday walks into the countryside, also under guard.

These latter were for recreation, a benefit again laid down in the Geneva Convention. As employers seldom felt it incumbent upon them to provide recreational facilities within the camp, it was not usually difficult to persuade the *Kommandant* to provide a guard to take ten or so prisoners for a Sunday afternoon walk.

Particularly was this the case as Red Cross parcels started to arrive regularly containing all manner of things such as chocolate, genuine coffee, genuine cigarettes and sundry other items which had long since disappeared from German military Commissariats and household larders. We were in a good position to offer enticing incentives.

Apart from acquiring in due time a useful map of Austria and Jugoslavia torn from child's school atlas and a small compass, both of which I still have, I was able, perhaps more importantly, to get a feel for the history and atmosphere of the region.

I acquired innocent seeming books from which I was able to study in some depth the history of both Austria and the Jugoslav peoples and understand the relationship between them all.

I was able to read the daily papers and listen to the radio newscasts. Although both of these were proud productions of Dr. Goebbels' Propaganda Ministry, there were nevertheless occasional items which could interest a scheming P.O.W. if he knew something of the background.

For instance, I read a couple of times in the press of the activities of a certain General Mihailovitch and his Serbian *Chetniks* who were apparently creating a minor nuisance for the Germans far to the south east. For a brief while it seemed that this could be the making of a nearer and more readily attainable goal. Alas! Mihailovitch's insurrection, representing as it did, Royalist Serbia, was doomed almost from the start. As such it could arouse no sympathy much less support among the Croats and Slovenes whose homelands occupied the north western portion of Jugoslavia and who wanted no resurrection of the pre-war state, based as it was on Serbian hegemony imposed by a hereditary Serbian king from the Serbian capital, Belgrade. Although the three peoples were Slavs of like ethnology speaking closely related languages, history had treated them differently.

The Croats and Slovenes were western in culture and Roman Catholic in religion; the Serbs, eastern and Orthodox. The Croats and Slovenes as subject peoples of the Austro Hungarian Empire had fought for the defeated Central Powers in World War I; Serbia, an independent kingdom had been on the side of the victorious Allies. Indeed it was the threatening posture taken by Austria towards Serbia that had precipitated that first global conflict. The Jugoslavia created at Versailles in 1919, whatever the intention of the great powers, rapidly became a Serbian empire. Belgrade regarded Croatia and Slovenia as conquered territories rather than federated and equal states.

Come 1941, many, perhaps a majority of Croats welcomed the German invaders with open arms - for years there had existed among them a strong and active, even if underground fascist party. The Germans quickly accorded them nominal independent statehood under their own *Poglavnik* or leader, Ante Pavelitch.

The Slovenes, in numbers, the smallest of the three major South Slav peoples, were also the most western in thought as well as geography. They were generally a more cultivated and less volatile people than their neighbours to the south east. Reabsorption into Austria they might possibly have accepted; but old Austria was now the *Ostmark*, a province of the Third Reich. Toward the German invaders, they were for the most part passively but definitely hostile. They felt that a properly constituted Jugoslavia in the government of which they were properly represented ought to be a workable proposition.

At all events Hitler spared the Slovenes no time to ponder but promptly incorporated the northern half of their lands into Greater Germany and tossed the other half to his jackal ally, Mussolini. The Slovenes actually came out of the 1941 invasion worse than either the Serbs or the Croats. The former preserved some sort of recognisable statehood under a local puppet government, the latter had their nominal independence. The Slovenes had neither statehood, land nor even shadow of autonomy. Even their status was that of subjects but not citizens either of Germany or Italy. Under these circumstances it seemed to me that Slovenes generally should be worthwhile cultivating.

Certain limited opportunities for this were available if one developed a sufficiently cautious approach. The border marches of southern Austria were quite liberally sprinkled with people of Slovene descent; they had remained there tilling their peasant soil or conducting their village businesses even after Versailles gave them in 1919, an ethnic homeland to which they could return. The local spoken dialect for Austrian and Slovene alike was a weird conglomerate of German and Slovene known as Windisch to those Austrians from further north who spoke only German.

Any useful relationship with these people had to be developed with great caution over a long period. The Germans were certainly not at any stage unconscious of the disaffected elements in their midst and their security agencies were accordingly numerically strong, efficient and all pervading. Apart from a well manned civil police force, there was the *Abwehr*, the *Wehrmacht's* military counter intelligence organisation. Worse still were the S.S. and S.D. (Security Service) whose business was the terrorising of conquered peoples who refused to accept their serfdom. The *Gestapo*, civilian arm of these forces, was also there in strength albeit less obviously. Furthermore, every occupied territory has its secret quislings and Slovenia was no exception.

Everything I did throughout my last two years of captivity was designed to project the image of a cheerful if somewhat chuckle headed British colonial who was bent on nothing more than making himself daily more comfortable and who, in furtherance of that end, had acquired an unusual fluency in the German language.

In March 1943 I was elected Camp Leader by my fellow detainees again in accord with the Geneva Conventions which reserve this right of election to every group of P.O.W. Although it confers seniority on the appointee, it also makes him responsible for all negotiations with the detaining power and answerable to that authority for all irregularities in the camp and all misdemeanours of his followers. I believe that, apart from a reasonable popularity, I was elected unopposed by my colleagues because of my perceived skill in negotiating advantageously with the Germans. They considered the German name for the appointment, "*Vertrauensmann*", literally Confidence Man, not inappropriate in my case.

Somewhere about this time, I began to hear from my carefully cultivated contacts of a new insurrectionary movement. Under a shadowy leader called Tito, a group known as Partisans was starting to cause the Germans significant trouble "down south" in Bosnia and the southern parts of Croatia and Slovenia. Apparently the Partisan movement did not operate as a cohesive military formation but rather as detached and widely separated "bands" of varying strengths operating under their own commands with loose general control from a central headquarters. I sensed that my Slovene informants were inclined to look with more favour on the Partisans than on the *Chetniks*. It seemed that the new movement was regarded as being nationalist Jugoslav rather than Royalist Serb.

Sure enough, in due course the German press began publishing the odd item about communist bandits operating in the remoter parts of the Balkans, stressing of course, that the Reich's security forces had wiped them out. As time passed, while still describing the insurrectionists as a communist rabble of insignificant numbers, the press acknowledged them by the name of Partisans and named their leader as Tito or rather Josip Broz, a Soviet agent with a long criminal record in pre war Belgrade. These repeated references to communist terrorists gave this particular Micawber the idea that something might be in the way of turning up.

Somewhere about this time Mussolini was dethroned and Italy, now invaded by the Allies, capitulated. Our camp strength which had fallen for various reasons to fifty four was now reinforced by the arrival of a group of British prisoners who had spent two years "in the bag" in Italy and who had now been taken over by the Germans. Our camp strength rocketed to about 100 again.

In September 1943 the Germans tired of our road building efforts and closed the camp, whereupon we were transferred back to Maribor to try our skill at re ballasting the railway line running west parallel with the Drava river to Klagenfurt and Villach. Maribor as I remember it was a pleasant little city of some 70,000 population on the northern bank of the Drava, a river wide and deep with a predictably strong current that only strong swimmers would tackle. I was, however, fascinated to note that the railway on which we were to work crossed the river at Maribor and that we would, although quartered in the town, actually be working some 12 miles west on the southern side of the stream.

Maribor was now a city of some military importance. It was a railway junction on the main line from Vienna to Italy and also from Vienna to Greece, Bulgaria and Southern Russia. Apart from this, it had a large aircraft factory on its south west perimeter. Being just south of the old border its inhabitants were mainly Slovenes and therefore suspect by the Germans. The place absolutely crawled with German security forces. In one day I was able to identify troops of three different S.S. formations as well as a couple of members of the S.D. When one realises the value that Hitler placed on these elite arms of his military machine, one can readily realise that no chances were to be taken with a few disaffected Slav "*untermenschen*" (subhumans). In retrospect I suppose it is the recollection of German arrogance vis a vis Slav peoples generally that still baffles me all these years after. How was it that millions of people of average intelligence and education could be seduced into believing that, because they hailed from the land between the Rhine and Oder rivers, they were members of a master race, designed by some vague Providence to have dominion over the rest of mankind? Their attitude to their Slav subjects was quite definitely far more arrogant and repressive than that of the Afrikaner towards the black African. At any given time the Germans held upwards of a hundred Slovenes in local gaols as hostages. For every German killed in a Partisan raid or for any considerable damage to communications and infrastructure in general, at least ten of these would be put through a caricature of a trial and solemnly sentenced to death. For maximum impact, the victims were allowed, immediately prior to execution, to write letters to their next of kin.

The following are translations of two poignant examples:- Good-bye letter written by Albin and Marjan Milavec. Albin, electrician, was born at Brezice in 1923; Marjan, student, was born at Brezice in 1924. The two were shot at Maribor on December 27 1941. Their brother Ivan, Partisan combatant of the Brezice Company, was killed in action on November 28, 1941.

Maribor, December 27, 1941
Dearest Parents,
Our last greetings go to you dearest dad and mum and brother France.
Forgive us and may you be happy, give our love to the boss, the Kral
boys and uncle. Marjan and I must die, today it'll be all over. Ivan has
already been killed in action.
Dearest Parents, God be with you!
A hug from Albin and Marjan

Goodbye letter written by Joze Fluks, workman, Maribor. He was born in 1920 and shot at Maribor on March 30, 1942.

March 30, 1942
Dear folks,
Today I was sentenced to death! Don't mourn for me, be brave as I am brave. In my thoughts I kiss you all, mum, dad, Majda, Jelka, Tony, my girl Ancka and all my friends and pals. Think well of me, I will think of you till the end. In my thoughts I send you my last kisses.
Joze

The executions were usually by machine gun fire with the victims lined up together against a wall. Six hundred and eighty nine Slovenes met their death in this fashion during the occupation in Maribor gaol alone. All told the Germans executed 1,590 Slovene hostages in their occupation area, including 82 women, the last mindless mass murder taking place at Maribor on 3 April 1945 when 18 men were gunned down.

To get further value for these atrocities by way of publicity each execution was advertised after the event by a rash of red posters on which were listed the victims' names, their "crime" and the place and date of the execution. The placards were displayed at every post office, railway station and town or village hall.

Among the victims was one Ivan Ferluga, a qualified engineer who had worked on the road construction job with us as a foreman.

Against such a background it was obvious that intense and delicate circumspection was to be of the essence at all times.

CHAPTER TWO
ESCAPE - IDEAS AND SCHEMES

There could be no doubt that the Partisans were making quite a marked impact on the road and rail communications in the southern and south western areas of Jugoslavia all the way from the Italian border down.

Well after the event I would learn that a party of them had ambushed a convoy or military train little more than 100 miles away. The Germans found the Partisans elusive, almost impossible to pin down. What chance did I have? The question was more than a rhetorical one. I wanted to escape and get back to my own lines. In a necessarily dangerous operation, I was seeking the safest road to success. It seemed to me that bands of local patriots waging irregular warfare against their foreign conquerors could be at least some help. By the beginning of 1944, I at last knew broadly what I would do. I would escape in full marching order as a British soldier wearing a British battle dress after I had somehow found some means of contacting Tito's men. Towards this latter end, I would step up my patient information gathering with a view to getting away in May or June. As most of the country I would be covering would be pretty well elevated, spring would need to be well advanced before this steep hill country was sufficiently clear of snow to allow a man in a hurry a reasonable passage on foot.

Little by little I garnered bits of information about the Partisans from Slovene tradespeople and peasants and even from the third hand gossip of our guards. One fact I did establish rather firmly: unarmed men in British uniform were not, ipso facto, welcomed by the Partisans. The Germans had used this particular form of Trojan Horse rather effectively in the past. Their English speaking agents dressed in our colours had gone into the hills and forests of the country and had been sheltered by Partisan agents or communities with dire results for these latter when the poseur eventually gave them the slip and returned to base. Be it said that the Germans and the Partisans were agreed on one thing: the Partisans took no prisoners; the Germans did so, if at all, only for the purposes of public demonstration and extracting information by torture before ultimate execution.

If I was going to join the Partisans it appeared that a formal and personal introduction would have to be arranged.

Up to this time I had never indicated to any of my colleagues that I was in any way thinking seriously of escaping. We all talked about it in a detached sort of way, but after three years most of the camp had come to accept the restrictions and limitations of our life style.

However, with the coming of spring, Partisan activity was renewed and I started to receive reports (well after the events) of raids by them one within fifty miles of Maribor. Something had to be done and done quickly. To me it seemed foolish even to hope that the Germans would continue to hold us there in a strategic centre which at the same time was so close to a region where hostile forces could raid and destroy. Several times I was given "possible probable" dates on which a raid would take place within sixty or seventy miles; but the information was always so sketchy and tentative as to be worthless. Remember the job I was planning was to be "all duck or no dinner" and it was likely to be "no dinner" for an escaping P.O.W. picked up by the S.S in vengeful pursuit of "communist bandits".

Lest one should believe that, at this point of time, (May 1944) the Germans were well beaten anyhow, let me remind the reader that the Normandy invasion was still only in prospect and in the event, a month later, turned out to be a perilously close thing. The Russians were in eastern Poland but showing no particular drive. In Italy the Anzio landing had clearly bogged down and the blood bath of Monte Cassino was still dragging to its bloody maw, thousands of candidates for martial and mortal glory. Be it also remembered that German morale was still such that August, 1944 registered the zenith of their armament production. No sign of weakness, no breech, no cracking appeared in the German security in southern Austria and north west Jugoslavia. Indeed with the intensified activity of Tito's bands, now air supplied at least to a limited extent by the RAF, German security forces quite definitely proliferated.

All of these considerations dictated to me that if I was going to make a break, it must be very soon. I was getting nowhere in my efforts to contact a real twenty four carat Partisan agent. I was largely confined to the camp and administrative business in Maribor. The railway job I visited, at most, once a week except when disputes between employer and prisoners arose. (Be it said that in these not infrequent situations, the guards took no part. Their business was firstly, to see that we did not escape and secondly to see that, in accordance with the Geneva Conventions we worked. At no time was it their business to adjudicate on the quality of our work. If, through language difficulties, the work was not being done to the employer's satisfaction, then it was the employer's business to have a registered and therefore non-working interpreter on the job. If he chose to save by having me, the sole official interpreter back in camp attending to administration, that was his business).

The job site was situated on the south bank of the Drava river in very sparsely settled mountain country a dozen or so miles west of Maribor - to be precise, in the vicinity of the hamlet, Ozhbalt. The prisoner work force was delivered thereto and returned therefrom daily by a special train consisting of a locomotive and passenger coaches. On delivery at either end, the train departed straightway to engage in whatever other business the German Railway had mapped out for it.

So from time to time, I visited the jobsite and one day - wait for it - the penny dropped. Could it be that lonely mountain country sparsely populated might be the place to find a Partisan scout? That night I confided my secret aims to one of the eight mates with whom I shared sleeping quarters - Driver Les Laws, Royal Engineers, an old timer who had been with the gang most of the way. He was a great chap and talented - a fine musician, fluent in French and well able (when he so desired) to get by in German with a bit of Slovene thrown in if required. Les had early decided that the niceties of relaying railways by physical human effort was not really his vocation. Somehow he sold the boss the idea that absenteeism, even of short duration could be curtailed, if a permanent supply of drinking water was always on hand for the thirsty workers. The foreman-in-chief bought the deal and from then on it was Les's job, supplied with a couple of wooden pails to trudge back and forth to the well at the only adjacent habitation, a railway signalman's cottage, and ensure that his colleagues did not faint from dehydration. At first, he did this under guard but, as time went on, vigilance relaxed as vigilance will and Les was soon making his quarter mile journeys up the hill unaccompanied. In these circumstances, it is not surprising that he soon developed a reasonably cosy relationship with the cottage family, Slovenes, of course.[4]

Thus far had the situation developed when Les and I first got together. I told him that I intended to make a successful break and to do so I wanted to contact the Partisans. Surely with his opportunities he should be able to find out something worth knowing. Why not pool our information as we came by it.

Les was a cheerful extrovert, older than the camp average, father of four children back in London. He expressed some surprise at my suggestion saying that he thought I was content to accept the status quo for the duration. He, on the other hand, was preparing to make a break at the earliest possible opportunity but like me, was trying to establish the facts about the Partisans. Were they really patriots fighting to free their country or were they, as the Germans claimed, criminal scum taking advantage of their country's plight to plunder, rape and destroy? He too was carefully trying to establish contact.

So we made a deal and agreed to pool information on the strict understanding that our plans remained a close secret between us.

This understanding was most important. Here we were among some 100 other prisoners, a considerable proportion of whom had, as already mentioned, come to terms, after three years, with our life style. Among this element escapes were not popular; escapes brought down on the camp a tightening of security, a reduction of hard won privileges, a stuffiness on the part of the Austrian guards with whom, generally speaking, we were on good terms. Escapes were invariably unsuccessful; why make life more miserable to no good purpose. Hard though it is to say it, there can be no doubt that any escape plans that came to expression outside the mind of the planner stood a good chance of being leaked to authority. There were too many instances of planned escapes having to be deferred or more often abandoned because our guards obviously "were in the know" for one to accept the matter as accident or coincidence.

By this time another appointment had come my way. I became the local Red Cross controller in charge of all Red Cross supplies for P.O.W. in the various camps scattered around the locality. These supplies came in bulk from *Stalag XVIIIA* Wolfsberg, Austria and were stored in a suitably secured building inside our compound. I had to distribute these goods, food parcels, clothing and medical supplies to the surrounding camps. Naturally I had to maintain a complete and accurate inventory of stock in my store and also keep a check list of all items in stock in the various camps which I supplied. Appropriate returns had to be posted off to *Stalag* weekly. It was quite a piece of work but I was happy to do it if only to keep my mind active.

A side benefit was that I had to know where the various camps I was supplying were located and what their "ration strengths" were. I also got to know my fellow camp leaders and was able to chat with them and pick up any gossip that was going when they made their periodical visits to my establishment to collect the Red Cross supplies due to their respective camps. This knowledge was, in due course, as will be seen later, to bear fruit.

As the Partisans continued to strike more frequently and more effectively, the local Slovenes became more openly disrespectful of their German overlords. So too did the German reprisals against them become more atrociously savage. The tension was building up to a pitch where something climactic was bound to happen. German *Abwehr* and S.D. searches of our camp became almost a commonplace.

The Allies had by now secured their foothold in Normandy and I determined that I would take my departure in August when the fruit was ripe on the trees and the harvest ripe in fields whether I had established liaison with the Partisans or not. Lest we were withdrawn from the area without warning I kept a rucksack of hard rations saved from Red Cross parcels stashed away in a safe place in the camp ready for an instant get away. I made sure that my boots were in first class order and my clothing in good shape.

Les Laws 1943

From cardboard and cloth cut from a worn out uniform I fashioned a peak which I sewed on to my forage cap to convert it to the style of headgear worn by Rommel's *Afrika Korps*. It was only a small detail but it nonetheless had quite a "germanising" effect on an otherwise completely correct British uniform. In a region where there were so many military and paramilitary formations, each with its own uniform I felt that this minor alteration of headgear, could, if necessary help me to move about among the population without being questioned unless I happened to run into professional security personnel. The more so was this the case as I spoke by now fluent colloquial Viennese German. I could even effect a German style of handwriting.

In any event my newly fashioned cap would be a minor disguise from people who knew me because I had managed to preserve my Australian slouch hat in wearable condition thus far and as I invariably wore it I was well known around the region as "the Englishman with the big hat".

Now July came in and with it the attempt to blow up Hitler in his eastern Headquarters. Something had to give. The Slovenes were bubbling and as they bubbled their information became wilder and less reliable.

It was in early July that our fellows started speaking of a civilian who had turned up on the job. He was not a worker - he would visit the workplace and talk with the guards and foremen for perhaps an hour or so and then disappear. I visited the workplace on one occasion while he was there and "listened in" while he was conversing with one of the guards and was able to make an informed guess that he was a Slovene because, though his German was fluent and colloquially correct, there was a telltale Slovene enunciation about it. The guards explained to me later that he was a forest warden from Laibach (Ljubljana) doing a survey of local timber resources. He earned the name of "Flash Harry" or sometimes "Harry the Bum" because of his habit of "bludging" a cigarette or two from our chaps on every visit. His intermittent visits continued for about a fortnight and then he disappeared.

Then one day Les Laws returned to camp with really startling news the sort of item that made one feel that one was living in the midst of a second rate paperback spy story.

Flash Harry was not just a bum. His name was Anton, and he was a relative of the young housewife whose well supplied our drinking water. He was also a Partisan agent. He had quietly accosted Les while the latter was coming from the house with his pails of water and spoken to him in German. He intimated to Les that he understood that he, Les, wished to get into personal touch with the Partisans. Well, he would be meeting three of them in a copse a couple of hundred metres from the job site the next day. Les could accompany him if he wished.

Next day I bit my finger nails down to the quick waiting for Les's return. His story when he arrived was short and to the point. He had met the three Partisans and although, as he said, they looked like something out of "Maid of the Mountains" there was no doubt that they were soldiers. They were armed with light machine pistols of a type Les hadn't seen before (Sten guns) and were heavily draped with ammunition bandoliers and hand grenades. They were doing a reconnaissance and expected to be raiding in strength within 35 kilometres of the job site in about three weeks.

Now at last here was something to plan on, now after two years of scheming and devising we had a deadline, a provisional D Day.

Now also the awkward questions started to arise. Les decided that in any escape he wanted his particular buddy to go with him. Be it said that in the P.O.W. set up almost all of us had at least one special buddy. Apart from matching personalities, and the need to have someone with whom to share thoughts, personal worries and news from home, there was the administrative angle. Red Cross food parcels and other supplies went further and made much better value if shared by at least two people; so, if for no other reason, we all had at least a recognised "partner" - some of these partnerships extended into syndicates of three and four. Naturally as many of these associations had endured for the whole period of our captivity, the bonds of mateship were very strong and the personal loyalties engendered, not lightly to be ignored.

So Les, with the break in immediate prospect, felt that his partner had to be in on the action. Les and I shared a barrack with six others, Andy Hamilton, a Scot, Ken Carson, an Australian, Griff Rendell, Bob McKenzie and Phil Tapping, all New Zealanders, and Len Austen a Tommy. The whole eight of us had been together for well over two years and considered ourselves together with, perhaps, a dozen or so other old stagers to be the hard core of the camp. It was noticeable that we were cleaner and tidier in our personal habits than later arrivals and we looked after our uniforms better and generally maintained a higher morale.

My seven barrack room buddies, were, at all events completely first class men who had preserved complete decency and dignity over the long years under circumstances that were never positively conducive to the maintenance of these highly desirable human qualities. They had all kept themselves in first class condition and any of them would be good company in a tight situation.

Andy Hamilton was Les's special buddy and although orthodox escapes were best done alone or in pairs, there was no doubt that what we were planning was going to be different. Neither Les nor I knew what the Partisans' ideas concerning us would be. Would they somehow guide us and assist us to the safety of the Allied lines in Italy or would they regard us as reinforcements, obliged by our common cause to join them in fighting the Germans and liberating their country? Although the former was the idea that both Les and I had in mind, we were nevertheless quite prepared to accept the latter if that was the way "the cookie crumbled". If Andy was prepared to take his chance with us, there could be no objection on my part. However, I took the opportunity to stake a claim for my long standing partner, Ken Carson. Very discreetly therefore we put the matter to them having admonished them to absolute silence. Neither hesitated for an instant; they were "in", pausing but briefly to curse us for being so devious and secretive with cobbers of such long standing.

Most Sunday mornings at 11 a.m. I usually called a parade of the whole camp for the purpose of making announcements and drawing attention to the various shortcomings of decency, hygiene, general good order and discipline whereby alone we could preserve health and dignity in our rough quarters. One of my favourite themes was the poor manner in which so many of the men turned themselves out. We all had good British battle dress uniforms provided for us at the expense of the taxpayer at home and delivered to us through the magical and magnificent agency of the International Red Cross. Why did so many shuffle off to the train in the morning clad in home made shorts, and other non uniform gear. Could they not wear their uniforms in public and change into their home made garments for work. Often I would have occasion to draw attention to the fact that the daily shave was being omitted by far too many of our number. Usually I would wind up with a summary of the week's news and a pep talk urging on all hands the wisdom of keeping bodies fit and spirits high in order that they might, in the fullness of time, return to families, wives and sweethearts in good shape to take up the challenges that the brave new post-war world would undoubtedly offer them.

I now realised that I must resign my position as camp leader in order to be on that job site every day. That was where the action was going to be; that was the place to which hard rations would have to be carefully smuggled and where all supplies would have to be cached.

After a year and a half of undisputed camp leadership it was difficult to tell the troops that I was stepping down without giving an intelligent reason. I would have to have a good story to tell *Herr Kommandant* also. As mentioned earlier, to have told my own men the real reason would have been a stupid breech of reasonable security without any basis of necessity. My position was further complicated by the personality of the *Kommandant, Unteroffizier* Johann Gross of Vienna.

During my *Arbeits Kommando* days *Kommandants* came and went at irregular intervals of about six weeks to two months. Most of them were ordinary middle aged sergeants, who were reasonable and, in the interests of a comfortable life for themselves, worked on the basis that if we behaved and gave them no trouble they would play it the same way. We did have, at different times, good samples of the genuine German "screaming skull" This was the type whom any irregularity or for that matter, any situation he didn't understand, was likely to send into a denture spitting, pistol waving, screaming frenzy. These usually hailed from Germany proper, they had a personal detestation for all enemies of the third *Reich* and passed up no opportunity for venting their feelings. To add to their frustration the guards they commanded were mostly Austrians who by reason of age or physical disability were unfit for front line duty. Austrians are quite properly renowned for their *"gemuetlicheit"*, a quality which has no exact translation in English but bespeaks an agreeable outlook and an acceptance of life as it comes. To the excitable German *Kommandants* such an attitude was intolerable in the middle of a war wherein the fatherland was fighting for culture and existence against the hordes of darkness that ringed it on all sides. Almost, it seemed, these middle aged logs of Austrians weren't interested in the war. Therefore *Herr Kommandant* would scream at his own guards with the same enthusiasm as that with which he screamed at us.

Naturally under this kind of command one had to walk warily. Any differences that arose between us and the employer as to fair working conditions were always resolved quickly in the latter's favour by the *Kommandant* sticking his automatic in somebody's ribs, (usually mine) and giving the prisoners thirty seconds to stop their complaining and resume work. An escape produced a really awesome result. The whole camp would be searched, our barracks left in complete disarray, anything of value or comfort to us was likely to be confiscated for a period and, (a favourite one, this) Red Cross supplies would be cut off. Any guard who may have been on duty at the time of the escape would be sent back to formation headquarters to enjoy seven days "bunker" on bread and water and a close physical examination to check whether he was not, after all, fit for duty at the front.

During the ten months we had been back in Maribor we had an entirely Austrian guard from the *Kommandant* down. Indeed the present commander who was now a consideration in my plans had been in charge for eight months. *Unteroffizier* Johan Gross was indeed a *"gemuetlicher"* Viennese. In appearance one would have sworn that he should have been caught in Hitler's first pogrom following the *Anschluss*. He was short and stocky with the classically hooked nose and dark beady eyes of the caricature Jew. The impression was heightened by the rimless pebble lensed spectacles which he affected. Our Londoners immediately nicknamed him "Whitechapel" and by this sobriquet he was known for the length of his stay with us.

His stated policy was the same as that of his predecessors "you behave, I'll behave etc." It didn't take me long however to spot a difference with the newcomer. Where the best of his predecessors had treated us with more or less detached tolerance seeking to maintain a neutral position between us and our employers, Gross obviously meant to see that we received a fair deal. Where other *Kommandants* considered it a nuisance when I sought their intervention to have the employer attend to a leaking barrack roof, or replace blankets long since worn out, or make good deficiencies in our rations, Gross made it his business to detect these things for himself and bring them to the contractors' notice and insist on prompt corrective action. Where his predecessors "went to water" on the occasions when *Abwehr* searched the camp, Gross would stay with the searchers, make an obvious inventory of anything that was taken away for further examination and insist on its return after it was cleared.

He also insisted on the searchers leaving our quarters as they found them instead of in the wretched mess that was their normal custom.

He gradually made it clear, by his attitude, that, whereas he had to maintain security and prevent our escape, he would do everything he could to make our detention as decent and comfortable as he could. He soon came to be both liked and respected by his charges and, working closely with him as camp leader, I came to know him very well and developed a really warm affection for him.

War is of itself, of course, a complete negation of all ethics, an abdication of the standards of acceptable conduct between man and man built up over the slow millenia during which our so called civilization has developed. In war the chap in the other uniform is the enemy and the fact that he may be a nice guy changes nothing. In action one seldom gets the chance to find out anyway. "Whitechapel" wore a German uniform and by maintaining an efficient even if benign guard over us performed the functions of a German soldier.

And yet and yet how was I, with what I could even then see developing, to leave this kindly decent, middle aged family man to take what would inevitably come his way. For eight months he had extended himself on our behalf. Four prisoners making a clean getaway would spell serious trouble for him. But how would it stop at four. How were Laws, Hamilton, Carson and I going to keep our plans from the other four old friends in our hut. When they found out, McKenzie, Rendell, Tapping and Austen would undoubtedly tag along with us whether invited or not. Who could tell what would eventually spill out of my scheming and plotting now that events were racing to a climax.

Micawber was becoming Hamlet. To return decency for decency and kindness for kindness or to tell myself that, as an Allied soldier, all persons in enemy uniform were my enemies to be treated as such without regard to any obligations moral or otherwise. Aye, there was the rub.

I took the punt and told Gross that he had been with us an inordinate length of time. I was resigning my position as camp leader so that our close personal relationship was at an end anyway. We had had a pleasant eight months together and for him to stay longer was simply to wait for the rough which must, in the natural order of things follow so much smooth. Surely having been in one command for four times the usual stretch he could reasonably seek a transfer.

Poor old "Whitechapel" was dumbfounded. Why was I resigning? Why should he leave? I could only inform him that what I was doing and what I was advising him to do seemed to me in the best interests of all concerned and that I was only telling him as much because I appreciated what he had done for us and wished our relationship to end on the same note of respect and friendship which had appertained for so long. He looked at me hard through his thick lensed glasses for some seconds. I returned the look with the best poker face I could muster. At last he said "Thank you, Mr. Camp Leader, I will do as you suggest". Three days later I shook hands with him and bade him goodbye as he left our camp and marched out of my life. Right up to that time we had always addressed each other by the formal German "*Sie*". He had always been "*Herr Kommandant*", I, "*Herr Vertrauensmann*" Now addressing me by my christian name and the intimate "*Du*", he bade me farewell, wished me luck and hoped that somehow I would remember him. I returned his compliments in similar fashion with all sincerity.

His successor quickly demonstrated that his attitude was the strictly orthodox one of a guard commander in charge of enemy prisoners. Strictest security again descended on the camp and the guards were ordered not to tolerate any slacking or indeed anything less than maximum effort on the part of work force.

However, the new "*Herr Kommandant*" remained my immediate personal problem for only a couple of days. On the first Sunday morning following his arrival, I called the usual Sunday parade and informed the troops that two years of fighting verbal battles on their behalf was as much as I or anyone else could be expected to take. To sound reasonably convincing I informed them that my nervous system had deteriorated to the point where my powers of negotiation were slipping. Furthermore my pleas for better discipline were being totally ignored as witness the fact that by and large they were now more than ever marching off to work like a rag tag rabble in their sloppy camp made garments instead of their uniforms as I had tried to insist. I was therefore, while thanking them for the confidence they had reposed in me, resigning my position with immediate effect.

There were protests from certain groups who had been in the camp a long time but by and large, I believe that the reasons for my resignation were accepted at face value and that no ulterior motives on my part were suspected by the camp as a whole.

I then called for the election of my successor and shortly thereafter, with feelings that Judas Iscariot would have understood, was handing over control, Red Cross stores and the camp leader's functions in general to Bob Shuttleworth, a cultured young English soldier whose command of German was flawless. Although he had only been with us a couple of months, he was obviously a very good style of young man who was only taking on the job because he felt it was his duty to do so.

I then waited on *Herr Kommandant*, announced my resignation and introduced Shuttleworth as the new camp leader. The commander, fortunately, regarded the niceties of the prisoners' own internal administration as being of only the slightest account and clearly did not interest himself in possible hidden factors.

On the Monday, correctly dressed in my British battledress with work shorts underneath I took my place in the ranks of the workers and marched off to catch our special train. In my camp made rucksack was a tin of bully beef, a block of chocolate and a packet of biscuits together with my old haversack. This was to be the nucleus of my hard rations to be cached "*in situ*" for the break that could not now be long in coming.

I was still by virtue of my easy Austrian German on terms of reasonable familiarity with most of the guards and although they were at first non-plussed by "Mister Camp Leader" overnight becoming one of the rank and file labourers, they accepted the situation as just another example of the inexplicable ways of the English in general and English P.O.W. in particular. My continued generosity with cigarettes, amply demonstrated that my personal attitudes had not changed. I was still the same comfortable, cheerful young chap as ever, still prepared to wait patiently for the war to end.

Planting my haversack wrapped in waterproof with its meagre contents on the first day in a well covered thicket seventy or eighty yards from the railway line presented no great difficulty. It only meant a couple of trips on the pretext of relieving myself in reasonable privacy. The haversack I concealed quite easily by covering it with dead twigs and bracken.

Day by day I added to the store until the haversack was reasonably full and therefore contained enough food to see me through for a fortnight if necessary. On two mornings my rucksack was searched as I paraded to leave camp, but I was able to explain without difficulty that I could not do a day's hard toil on the lousy German rations and therefore had to augment these latter from my own supplies. Indeed I was able to work up a fine show of indignation at the injustice of it all.

But as each day dragged out its weary course the tension mounted. Our state of mind was obviously starting to show. McKenzie, Rendell, Austin and Tapping were becoming increasingly aware that big things were afoot. The merest loose word, the slightest deviation from customary action and the camp would be buzzing with rumour. Abe Lincoln never spoke more truly than when he said "you can't fool all of the people all of the time". Where the great majority of the camp had accepted my recent demission at face value, at least a few of the old hands who knew me well must, in the boredom of their existence, have pondered the possibility of deep laid schemes, by that downy bird, "The Crow".

After several brief discussions with Les Laws in such little privacy as the camp offered, we decided, albeit reluctantly to tell our four remaining hut mates what was afoot and count them in. In the short space of four weeks my escape plans had expanded from a solo job, to a twosome, to a foursome and now to an eight man affair. This, if it came off, invoked a rather unpleasant technicality. Whereas the Germans accepted that escaping was a P.O.W.'s duty, they made it clear that they did not consider it a P.O.W.'s duty either to incite or assist his fellows let alone lead them in this purpose. According to a large notice printed in both German and English posted in their P.O.W. camps, German military law regarded the contemporaneous escape of seven prisoners or more as mass escape which was, under that law, construed as mutiny. The ring leader of a mutiny in the German army was subject to the death penalty on conviction by Court martial. The notice referred to above made it clear that the leader of a mass escape of P.O.W. would be similarly proscribed.

This being so I certainly had the highest incentive to ensure that our escape was completely and ultimately successful. I could not see the Germans looking past me to find the ring leader of this particular exercise.

This thought led me to the further consideration that if I was going to commit myself to this extent, why not go the whole hog and take the entire camp. The Partisans were getting bolder by the week, we had our personal introduction to them (we hoped). Why not?

On reflection, of course, this was impossible. Ninety to a hundred men who had known no real military drill or discipline for three years would cruel the chances of a smaller party. The going would obviously be tough and a lot of the men were not in as good a shape physically as they might have been. How, in the pursuit that would obviously take place, could I hope to maintain control of so large a party marching through mountainous terrain heavily occupied by elite enemy troops. The more so was this the case when one realises that we would be dependent for rations on what we could forage as we went.

No. An impossible dream, but still somehow I could not help regretting that I would, in a way, be deserting a fine bunch of fellows, a large number of whom had given me their rough and ready confidence and friendship for upwards of two years. Nevertheless commonsense dictated that eight was an amply big enough risk to run. Ninety, impossible.

By now I had become a well practised observer of German military activity and, watching the various formations of S.S. and ordinary troops entraining at Maribor station on south bound lines, it was obvious that military activity in the Balkans was being stepped up. Two months before the local newspapers had been full of an account of the destruction of Tito's headquarters in Bosnia. Allegedly, airborne German forces supported by tanks and aircraft for which the guerillas had no counter had launched a massive attack, which, while it failed to capture the "bandit chief", had nevertheless wiped out his best troops, wrought havoc with his communications and taught his civilian supporters a lesson which the limited number of survivors would not lightly forget. One paper even carried pictures of paratroopers holding up items of female underwear said to have been found in Tito's personal quarters. Naturally the usual tendency toward journalistic smut by Goebbels' press was given free rein.

Maribor, as I have said was a railway junction feeding Italy, Greece and, if need be, the southern Russian front. The upsurge, both in numbers and movement of these security forces strongly suggested that the Germans were strengthening their lines of communication either to reinforce their troops in those areas, or possibly, to evacuate them. This latter was a distinct possibility in the south east. The Russians were now invading Bulgaria, thus threatening the Germans in Greece and Serbia with an outflanking movement. Were it not for Hitler's crazy insistence on defending every scrap of ground to the last man and the last round it seemed that the Germans could well withdraw from Greece and the lower Balkans without damaging their war effort and give themselves a shorter front on which to deploy their defending forces. This would also rid them of the nuisance of disaffected civilian populations waging very effective guerilla campaigns against their lines of communication.

In any event, Maribor was unlikely long to remain a safe area in which to hold P.O.W. for whatever reason; I didn't really need a Lady Macbeth to remind me to "stand not upon the order of your going but go at once". Fortunately I had the good sense to keep all this kind of thinking to myself. Laws and I waited until after lock up that night (a Friday I seem to remember) and then told our four remaining colleagues of our plans and invited them to join us. All accepted with alacrity. I, on the other hand, went to sleep that night knowing that another week must see me on my way. I had been "one of the mob" for almost a fortnight now. I was fit, well provisioned; I had a map and compass. With or without help from the Partisans I must make the break during the following week.

Monday came - back to work and even more urgent expectation only to have the day pass maddeningly slowly without any break in the dreary routine. Back in our barrack room eight edgy conspirators looked at one another with little to say. Each shared the others' frustration. Tuesday night after lock up Les informed us that Anton had spoken to him briefly that afternoon and told him to "stand by" for early action; things were moving. Next morning after washing and shaving I slipped one of my precious "*Solingen*" blade razors and my toothbrush into my hip pocket and despite the bright August weather, pulled on heavy long underpants, a warm singlet, heavy shirt and a pullover prior to donning my battledress, thick socks and heavy soled boots.

Down to the railway station we marched, waited a few moments for our two carriages to pull in and then "all aboard". The light locomotive puffed slowly out of the station, clanked noisily across the railway bridge over the Drava and we were on our way - for the last time?

Chapter Three
The Small Escape

At the little siding of Rushe, we stopped to drop our cook, the New Zealander, "Shorty" Humm who cooked our midday meal there. This purpose quickly fulfilled, the train rattled on another 10 miles or so to the worksite. Out we climbed, and in response to the shouting of the civilian overseer and his foremen, set to work in our usual muddling and casual fashion.

Soon it was morning smoko; Les Laws was looking blank. He had been up to the farm house for water twice but Anton was no where in evidence. Back to toil - what was going on? Was anything? Go today! Go while you can! Yes, speak to Ken Carson at lunchtime and tell him. He can come too if he wishes. Lunch time came and with it Les, quietly going the rounds. Anton had met him in a copse near the cottage and told him that the Partisans had captured and would hold for 24 hours the village of Lovrenc 10 km away. I had spotted it on the map previously. It was situated to our southwest in remote hill country difficult of access. No main road or railway apparently went near it. The Partisans had moved into it to display their strength to the local civilians and to flush out any pro German elements they might find there. Owing to its isolation, Lovrenc could well be held for 24 hours or more because it would be all of that time before the nearest German troops could counter attack in sufficient strength.

We were to rendezvous under a big chestnut tree some two hundred yards from the railway, at the foot of the western slope of the hill on which the cottage stood at four o'clock that afternoon. Anton would be waiting for us.

At last it was on!

Afternoon smoko three o'clock.

My seven colleagues all looking and (to me) behaving like guilty men. Hell, Churches, what's making you so jumpy and tense? You're well prepared, nothing can go wrong. Three forty five, McKenzie and Rendell were missing, Hamilton and Carson both tall men were slouching off to the bushes each with a sheet of paper ostentatiously in hand. Laws was trudging up the hill with his water pails (hopefully for the last time). Austen had "gone sick" at smoko and I had last seen him lying in the shade of some bushes thirty yards from the line. Doubtless he was on his way. Tapping had the misfortune to be working with a gang on a stretch of track some 100 yards from where I was. Here the line entered a minor cutting which although only perhaps twelve feet high, nevertheless made it difficult for Phil to excuse himself for the usual reason. If one wanted to go to the latrine why climb a cutting when there were suitable thickets on the river side of the line.

I could delay no longer. I casually walked up the slope and retrieved my haversack from its hiding place. I had just slung it over my shoulder when - hell and damnation - there was one of the guards walking purposefully towards me. This was definitely a time for quick thinking. Was my secret out? Had the guard been alerted? No use to run for it. I wouldn't make it and it would louse it up for the others. I waited for the guard to approach; he seemed quite normal. This was old Gustl Breithof. He had been with us some three months and was quite easy going. He readily accepted minor handouts in the way of cigarettes and soap and had been on at least one "black marketing" Sunday walk with me during which he had been quite complacent and accepted due reward for his "*gemuetlichkeit*". He was a native of Bolzano (Bosen) in the Alto

Adige (South Tyrol). He had been expatriated under the arrangement whereby Hitler, in ceding this disputed territory to his stooge Mussolini, had claimed some of the inhabitants of German stock and taken them into the fatherland lest their continued presence on their native soil create untoward incidents with the ruling Italian Fascists. Breithof was a peasant and therefore not exactly Hitler's most enthusiastic soldier.

Nevertheless, I had to do something and quickly. "Gustl, old boy", I said patting my haversack, "at the house up there they have plenty of eggs and I'm just on my way to do a little business. I fancy eggs for tea myself; stick around and I'll cut you in for a couple, O.K.? Here, have a decent cigarette while you're waiting" at the same time handing him a packet with two cigarettes in it.

Glory be! Gustav smiled; he'd seen that haversack loaded with trade goods before. He agreed that eggs (scarce and strictly rationed) would be just right for supper and I was on my way.

Up by the cottage down the western slope of the hill and there was the chestnut tree. It was four o'clock exactly. All the party were there with the exception of Tapping and all were getting worried. Anton for obvious reasons wanted to get going in order to make Lovrenc in daylight. In the rough country we had to traverse it would be all of a two hour march.

Bearing in mind Tapping's dilemma as I had last seen him, I gave the nod to start.

We made off along the steep bush track leading into the mountains in the warm bright light of a sunny afternoon. The day was Wednesday; the date was the thirtieth of August 1944.

And it was indeed that glorious weather for being out of doors which central Europe at its kindest offers in late summer. Nor did the Styrian countryside lack anything in woodland serenity. Somehow I recall no sense of the tension, the jitters that had been with me in increasing degree for the last few days and which had come close to betraying me in the last couple of hours had evaporated. No! Somehow what we were doing right then, tramping through beautiful woodland in warm late summer sunshine seemed a completely logical, appropriate and normal thing for seven healthy young men to be doing without any reference at all to the earnest purpose which motivated our marching.

However, pleasant though the conditions beyond doubt were, the way to Lovrenc was up, decidedly up - up into the hills which mark the final descent of the Julian Alps to the plains where the Drava and Sava rivers flow to their ultimate conjunction with the Danube.

Wearing, as we were, our entire wardrobes battledress, pullover shirt and fleecy underwear, two miles of brisk walking in warm sunshine was enough to bring us to sweaty saturation. Our guide was lean and tireless and spared us just enough time to peel off down to trousers and shirts and stash the surplus clothing in our packs. We must make Lovrenc in daylight.

Peasants' cottages with barking dogs must be carefully avoided, involving a certain amount of detouring and more kilometres but all in a good cause.

It was just on seven o'clock; from my school atlas contour map I knew we must be nearing our goal when into our path stepped a young man in German uniform with a tommy gun which he levelled at us quite firmly. "*Stoj*", he said. Ah! blessed relief. Had the uniform been original issue he would have said *"Stehen geblieben"* or something similarly and germanically unpleasant. *"Stoj"* was Slovene for "Halt".

Anton quickly identified himself and us. Without pausing long I noticed that the young man with the tommy gun had a red five pointed star stitched on the front of his forage cap in place of the German roundel. We had, for good or ill, reached the Partisans.

On we went but now every couple of hundred yards we were similarly bailed up and identified. Obviously Partisan security was organised and efficient. Gradually, almost without noticing it, we were out of the woodlands and the valley meadows which ran with them and found ourselves on a narrow macadam road between a straggle of cottages which betokened the approach to a township. Minutes later we were in the middle of the little town of Lovrenc under the curious eyes of groups of armed Partisans and small knots of townsfolk whose expressions ran the gamut from terror through indignation, apprehension, nervousness to satisfaction, joy and national pride depending on their political colour and the degree of patronage or persecution they had received from the recently ousted Germans.

The Partisans by their dress certainly merited Les Laws' description of a "Maid of the Mountains outfit:" more impressively kitted stage brigands I never saw; the preponderance of uniforms was the field grey green of the German army; then there was the brown of the German *Arbeitsdienst* (roughly, labour corps). The darker blue grey of the Italian army was well represented and, unbelievably, in about half a dozen cases the dove grey of the Royal Jugoslav army which Hitler had decimated in 1941. The sole common identification was that five pointed red star on the forage cap. Some had crossed bandoliers over their shoulders bearing ammunition pouches.

Some carried their ammunition on waist belts. All appeared to have hand grenades attached to their persons and carried them with a nonchalance that made me, for one, rather nervous. Among them to our surprise was a scattering of young women similarly garbed and armed who, it eventuated, served for the most part as medical orderlies, neither seeking nor accepting consideration because of their sex. Maybe it was the reaction of three years to the life monastic but I don't recall seeing one girl Partisan who did not look pretty and who did not wear her made over uniform in comely fashion and well.

Anton's credentials must have been quite sound because within quarter of an hour of our arrival we were in the village "*gostilna*" drinking *slivovitz* with two pleasant young men whose well made over German uniforms and polished riding boots betokened their officer status. Double thin red stripes on their epaulettes suggested that they were lieutenants and this turned out to be the case. With them was a third young man, who, while lacking the stripes of rank, had a red star, five pointed naturally, on either upper sleeve immediately below the shoulder. Though without particular rank, he obviously "rated". Yes, indeed, this was the political commissar without whom, apparently, no Partisan formation, worthy of any note at all, could be considered complete.

None of these three spoke German. So Anton had to act as interpreter. The formation which we had joined were not locals. They were from Lower Carniola (Bela Krainj) in the far south east of Slovenia.

Exactly why they were operating there in the extreme north a hundred miles or more from home I was unable to establish.[5] Partisans usually operated in their native locality where they had the advantage of complete familiarity with the terrain. The senior of the two lieutenants was a brigade commander while the junior was in command of the "battalion". This latter consisted of the force now holding Lovrenc, about a hundred strong.

They had already held Lovrenc for twenty four hours during which time they had seized the local police station and locked up the six constables in their own cells and naturally taken possession of the armoury. They had also done some recruiting among the fit young townsmen.

Apart from this they locked up the local civil authorities and made a bonfire of all civic and police records. There had been a couple of public meetings in the town square at which the commissar had been able to spell out to the locals the niceties of communist dogma and paint a glowing picture of the glories in store for all when the gallant Partisans had defeated the might of Germany, liberated the land forever and created a fit place for Tito to set up his rosy red communist paradise.

Nevertheless, the military commanders were obviously well trained guerillas and never allowed themselves to forget that their war was a war of constant movement. Capturing a township or a given strong point was one thing, holding it long enough to become a target for the overwhelming might of the vengeful Nazis was quite another. Close as they were to so strongly held a spot as Maribor, their tenure of Lovrenc would be very brief indeed. The principal object of the exercise was to indoctrinate the locals and let them know that, as loyal Jugoslavs, they had a national army in the field which had considerably more striking power than the German controlled newspapers circulating in the area had led them to believe. Having done this they planned to be off next day and would happily take us with them.

Food was brought and over the meal washed down with local riesling and more slivovitz we enquired as to what they could do to expedite our journey to the sunny climes of southern Italy where the Allied forces were now in unchallenged occupation. At this our new found friends became a little hazy and spoke vaguely of British and American officers operating with the Partisans "further south". Our movements could be better decided "further south".

By this time, under the heady influence of freedom and the extreme cordiality of our welcome we decided that sufficient progress had been made for one day. For some time we had been aware of music and gaiety abroad in the town of Lovrenc The sound of concertina and fiddle with voices raised in song was borne to us strongly if not altogether blithely on the cool night air. This, accompanied by a rhythmic stomping, suggested that the Styrian version of a "*schuh plattler*" or clog dance was being performed and enjoyed by the present populace of the sequestered settlement.

The commander suggested that we might look in on the festivities and led us to the local hall to watch. Very quickly I found myself stomping my hardest to keep in time with a junoesque Partisan lass in a measure that, for vigour and improvisation would surely have made the Cornish Floral Dance seem like a stately eighteenth century gavotte.

Ten minutes of this sort of activity, again fully clad, and I was once more in a lather of perspiration. I thanked my energetic partner and bowed out. I engaged some of the locals in conversation while I cooled down. It was an illuminating experience. National pride and their detestation of the Germans naturally tended to make them strongly pro Partisan; against this was their strict Roman Catholic religion with its ban on everything which that five pointed red star stood for. The long term hope of permanent liberation and the restoration of their nationhood mingled with fear of the reprisals which the Germans on re-occupation a couple of days hence would exact; overlaying these considerations was the imponderable problem of whether, upon the realisation of their long term hopes, they would be able to "render unto Caesar the things which are Caesar's and unto God the things that are God's".

I could only remind them that almost nothing could be worse than their present state of vassalage - subjects but not citizens and that their best course was to assist the Partisans by all means available. Following the final eviction of the Germans they could then expect to participate, at least to some extent, in the civil government which the Partisans would set up after the war. I had already come by the feeling that the Royal Jugoslav Ministry housed in far away London was not going to figure very strongly in the immediate post war governing of Jugoslavia. Tito and his scattered bands had endured unspeakable hardships and cruel casualties in their guerrilla campaign. With the final defeat of Germany the Partisans would be de facto, the rulers of the country with Tito, Chief of State. Any power however strong which wished to prevent that "de facto" from becoming "de jure" would be well advised to compute the profit and loss statement as regards both men and material well in advance.

Yes! Any power. Even the U.S.S.R. to which Partisan political ideology was naturally slanted and to which these sturdy patriots looked for inspiration if not as fellow communists, at least as fellow Slavs? Oddly I had noticed an incident on our arrival in the hall. The commander had noticed one of the Partisans wearing a red star brooch on his tunic. On the red star was superimposed the hammer and sickle. He spoke sharply to the man who quickly removed the badge. I understood the language well enough to understand "You are a Jugoslav soldier not a Russian".

Deep and fundamental problems awaited Jugoslavia on the morrow of victory, too complex for a simple Australian blessed with a continental homeland having only the oceans to delineate its boundaries. Home! Was I really on my way? Would I make it? Having seen the Partisans' discipline and morale I was already convinced that I would.

With a hundred well armed, well led soldiers guided by locals who knew their countryside as intimately as a suburbanite at home knew his own back garden how could we miss? Even seven of us seemed a lightweight effort now that I was able to see the realities with my own eyes. How were the blokes back in camp at Maribor faring? They would have been locked up for the night long since. What sort of ruckus had taken place at evening roll call with seven of us missing? A good bunch of blokes those: my party's escape would probably write an early "*finis*" to the present railway job: it would probably mean the evacuation of the whole camp to more secure areas further north. Whatever happened security would be ruthlessly tightened and treatment would inevitably become more rigorous.

Was it real compassion and comradeship for those left behind? Was it "dutch courage" generated by the slivovitz and riesling? I doubt I shall ever know now. I decided that I must have a further talk with the Partisan commanders. I looked for Anton to do some interpreting for me. He was nowhere to be found. Like the good cloak and dagger man he was, he had quietly disappeared. We never saw him again.

However I soon found one of the local townsmen who was happy to help. We sought out the two officers and I got quickly down to business. They did not consider escorting seven unarmed escapees too much of an impediment or embarrassment? No! On the contrary they were delighted to help any Britishers if only in return for the material help which the British were now giving the Partisans by way of air dropped supplies of ammunition and equipment. Could they handle a larger party? Oh yes, that should be possible.

How much larger party? Please what, if anything, did I have in mind?

I then explained to them the exact situation back at the job on the railway line. The normal working party there consisted of some 80 prisoners like us, guarded by a dozen or so middle aged guards with World War I repeating rifles. Also present were some five civilians to direct our labours. It was a comparatively lonely spot well away from habitation. Would they be able to make a raid and release our comrades and guide them "further south" as they proposed to do with us?

This was obviously quite a question one that needed thought and consultation. The two of them discussed it between themselves at some length. Once again my knowledge of Slovene was too sketchy to follow the discussion exactly but I was able to pick up certain points: Firstly the exercise was a desirable one and its successful execution would bring some kudos to this particular Partisan unit. Secondly it would delay their departure from the region by some eight hours, a possibly dangerous delay. Thirdly the whole thing could be a cunningly devised German trap.

However, after ten minutes or so the interpreter and I were drawn back into the centre of things. Yes they would be happy to do as I suggested provided I and one other member of my party would accompany the Partisans back to the work site to give instant assurance to our comrades and thus forestall possible panic among them.

I saw the point and expressed my pleasure at their decision and my willingness to play my part. I then went off and told my fellows what was afoot and suggested Les Laws as the other half of the assurance and anti-panic department.

This new development was viewed at first with some concern by my party who understandably considered that we were already playing our luck hard enough. However doubts were quite quickly overcome and I was soon back with the Partisan commander to inform him that we were ready when he was.

As the idea of eighty odd "guests" did not seem to worry our hosts, I mentioned as a further thought, that there was a party of nine British prisoners working from a farming camp some ten miles this side of Maribor. I knew its exact location from my recent job of chief Red Cross storeman distributing supplies to the various camps in the area.

This camp, actually an old farm cottage, was in a rural setting some hundreds of yards from the nearest habitation and was in charge of a single guard. If Comrade Commander really didn't object to the number of escapees he took in tow then this farm camp should be a simple enough target for a quick raid. The young lieutenant thanked me for the information but gave no indication of whether he intended to act on it.

Next there was a technicality, a side issue but nevertheless too important a problem in my mind to be left unresolved. What did Comrade Commander propose to do with the guards who would fall into his hands as a result of the exercise? At this the young man smiled enigmatically and asked me for my suggestions. He pointed out that the German forces took Partisan prisoners if at all, only to torture information out of them; having served this purpose, the hapless victims were then executed either by hanging or shooting. The German security forces accepted that they could scarcely look for quarter from the Partisans and tended when engaged in battle to fight to the death rather than be captured.

I pointed out that the operation which we were now considering was somewhat different. Instead of the young, fit, hard bitten, Nazi zealots of the S.S. and S.D. we would be confronted only by a negligible force of middle aged Austrian guards unfit for front line duty and perhaps five civilians some of whom were Slovenes anyway. They were quite decent inoffensive people who never had and never would do anybody hurt or violence if they could avoid it. There was not, in my view, the remotest possibility of them attempting the slightest gesture of resistance. Without being squeamish neither I nor my companions wished to be involved in any unnecessary bloodshed particularly where the victims were people whom we knew and with whom we were on cordial terms despite the technicality of our wearing opposing uniforms.

Comrade Commander considered this for a brief while and then stated that, so long as there was no resistance and so long as the captives gave complete co-operation, they would march with us for a couple of days and then be turned loose to find their own way back to base.

Having cleared this worrisome point, I felt that it was time to call it a day. By now it was midnight, 18 hours since reveille with a lot of physically and mentally exhausting activity in between. To be back on the job site by 8 a.m. to "meet the train" we would need to leave Lovrenc by 5:30 a.m. so that if we were going to get even as little as five hours sleep it was high time to get our heads down. We therefore found a heap of straw in a shed and wasted no time getting off to sleep.

CHAPTER FOUR
THE BIG BUST

I had hardly closed my eyes it seemed when I was awakened by the usual sounds of a camp coming astir. As I had only taken off my hat as a token of, undressing, "getting up" was, on this occasion, literally just that. I didn't even have to throw back the blankets. It was quarter to five and the troops were making ready for the march.

I quickly roused Laws and, pausing only to sluice the sleep out of our eyes at the village pump, cast around in the dark to find out what the next move was. We soon found our way to the spot where the cook was serving a quick breakfast. The meal turned out to be maize meal porridge ungarnished by either sugar or the bacon fat which was the more common flavouring medium in those parts. It wasn't the most uplifting breakfast with which I've started a day but as I understood it, when one went campaigning with the Partisans one ate what was available as and when it came up. In this spirit, I accepted as well the goodly chunk of black bread which was also handed out. This latter staple it seemed would have to keep me going through the day.

This done, we were taken to join the column now forming up. To my surprise the two lieutenants were mounted, each on a very respectable looking horse, each horse harnessed with quite impressive saddle and bridle. This was real World War I infantry stuff - officers ride, troops march; not too much of egalitarian communism about this. However no time for ideological reflections; at least the young commissar was on foot with the rest of the troops. Then "*naprej*", Slovene for "advance" and we were away in single file back down the same track by which we had reached Lovrenc the previous evening. I marched alongside the Commander's left stirrup.

Shortly it was daylight. A five minute halt was called and the column rested up in a convenient copse. Our young Commander knew his business and, with the coming of daylight, broke the party up into sections of about ten men each. From then on the party moved in bounds from one piece of woodland to the next. a section at a time. The early appearance German *Fieselier Storch* light reconnaissance aircraft confirmed the wisdom of these tactics. At all events we must have kept moving because we were back at the chestnut tree rendezvous of the previous afternoon by twenty to eight.

The officers dismounted, tethered their horses and then moved the troops carefully and quietly over the final two hundred yards to the railway line. I indicated to the Commander the approximate centre point of the section of the railway on which we were working. I then went with him to both ends of the work site so that he knew the exact length of front he would have to cover.

As the stretch of railway line in question was only about two hundred yards in length and as he had close to a hundred men with him I was able to feel that he had our front in this particular action particularly well covered. In point of fact he shrewdly deployed about a third of his force under good cover in the trees about a hundred and fifty yards to the rear doubtless as a hedge against surprise.

In the middle of the site was, as I mentioned earlier, a small cutting which rose ten or twelve feet above the line at its highest point. It was here that the leader and I went to ground. Laws and the other lieutenant were some fifty yards away to our left. Those troops not covered by the cutting were naturally down on the level of the track and were therefore dependant for cover on such grass and bush as was available as well as the small stacks of railway ties usually found on a reballasting job. By five to eight all of us were down on our stomachs and hopefully under reasonable cover from first glance if not from intense scrutiny.

Eight o'clock came and went, a minute more, two minutes and then a distant rumble. The train was now approaching. Well! Everything normal so far. Another few minutes and the locomotive appeared round the bend a couple of hundred yards away puffing its way up the grade and trailing its carriages behind it. Another minute and it had ground to a halt in front of us. Guards, prisoners and civilians alighted in the wonted sluggish fashion. Shortly one of the guards gave the driver the "all clear" and the engine slowly started in reverse pushing the carriages back down the track to Maribor.

I watched, my chaps starting towards the tool boxes in the usual unenthusiastic style; the head foreman was bellowing his usual encouragements and admonitions, the guards were spacing themselves along the track with their rifles slung.

By the time I had taken all this in, the train was disappearing round the bend. The Commander, whistle in mouth, nudged me gently, I nodded my head and the whistle blew!

A split second later we were all on our feet amid the most frightening din. The Partisans shouting "hands up" in German, Italian and presumably Slovene. Wearing my Australian slouch hat for quick recognition I was bellowing with all my lung power "Get up here you bastards, at the bloody double" and then screaming to the guards in German with equal vigour to get their hands up and not to do anything that looked like possible resistance.

As a military operation it was flawless. In less time than it takes to write, our fellows were up among us. Les Laws and I moved down on to the track to encourage the guards to take it easy and hand over their arms to the Partisans who were even now moving among them. Then it was up, up and away. I suppose it could not have been two minutes from the whistle blast that we were moving back into the trees where the Partisan reserve was waiting.

I will not pause here to describe the various reactions of individuals to what had happened. Naturally surprise had been complete and surprise depending on its nature usually brings with it a greater or lesser degree of shock. The guards and civilians were obviously and predictably apprehensive, some of the released prisoners of war, quick on the uptake were elated, some dazed and confused.

However, no time was available for explanations. The two officers were already mounted. Once more, the command "*Naprej*" rang out and we were again on the march in single file back into the hills. After a couple of miles it became apparent that we were not retracing our footsteps. Enquiry elicited briefly that we were not returning to Lovrenc; rather we were heading roughly due south thereby leaving that village somewhere to the west.

Obviously the Partisans were bent on making up the eight hours which they had lost in carrying out the rescue operation. We swung along at a cracking pace without pauses for rest. This was a forced march with which British soldiers of generations past would have been well acquainted. Four hours of this brought us to a large farmstead at the head of a secluded valley. The column halted thankfully for rest. Now I had time to count the heads. Firstly we were rejoined by Carson, Hamilton, Rendell, McKenzie and Austen who had been escorted across country from Lovrenc. In the raid we had released 79 prisoners, and captured 8 guards and four civilians. I was delighted to notice among the party so many of my original gang from the road building days at Shentilj. Among the Tommies there were "Snowy" Brooker of the British regular army, gentlemanly Ken Dutt and his buddy Hank Dale, the camp comic; Bert Avis and Reg Allen, "Pug" Vickers and Taffy Evans from Wales and Joe Ferznolo from London. Phil Tapping, the Kiwi who had "missed the bus" the previous afternoon, was there, so too was Henari Turangi, the ever cheerful Maori. Of my fellow Australians I recall clearly Don Funston, the large and carefree Victorian corporal, Bill Gossner the ex New Guinea planter, Stan Broad N.Q. and Jim Woods from Melbourne.

The next quarter hour was quite naturally a period of bubbling babbling explanations with questions being fired at the original seven and at me in particular from all sides all at the same time. I took time out to tell the guards and civilians from the railway that, so long as they went along and did not try any heroics, they would be quite safe. The chances of these amiable middle aged men trying to win an Iron Cross from Hitler in a cause for which they had never been in any way enthusiastic would have been a bookmaker's delight so I was not really worried. Nevertheless, having been stuck up by "communist bandits" whose reputation for summary dealing with such members of the *Wehrmacht* as fell in to their hands had been given such wide publicity and having, in addition, been forced to cover some fourteen miles in four hours, they were certainly in need of some reassurance.

Somehow I guess that they backed their judgment of me and accepted my assurances at least as a basis for hope if not as a complete guarantee. One or two of them told me with rueful smiles that I was a "*grosser Gauner*" (a great rogue) but in best Austrian tradition they accepted the situation as being one that they could not alter and awaited developments. I had rather more pressing problems on my mind, however, than the hopes and fears of my late captors even granting that I was quite well disposed to them. Only about a half of the party whom we had released were wearing their uniforms. Many were clad only in shirts, home made shorts, boots and socks, the same old working outfits to which I had made so many caustic references back in camp at Maribor.

I had no means of knowing just where the Partisans might take us and by what route we would march but I did have an idea that, as practised guerrillas, they would travel the most rugged and inaccessible country possible. For our safety I certainly hoped so. Rugged and inaccessible country in north western Slovenia was mountain country rising in parts to six and seven thousand feet. I had a feeling that a lot of my troops were going to be very cold before they were much older.

Nor was clothing their only lack.

While we were talking a thick soup was being served from the farm washboiler. This was great except for one thing - our people carried their cutlery with them to the worksite but their dixies were back at the cook house. How to serve soup to ninety odd people who did not have a receptacle between them? This was eventually resolved by borrowing from the Partisans after they had partaken. This created the further problem of stretching out the time necessary to get everyone fed and I was under no illusions concerning the value of time so far as we were concerned.

We were still not more than 20 miles from Maribor and, unless my appreciation of the situation was wildly astray, news that a large band of Partisans had raided right up to the Austrian border would already be known to the Germans there. Bearing in mind that, in 1938 the world accepted Hitler's annexation of Austria, the raid in which I had taken part had brought a recognisable hostile military force right to the sacred frontiers of the Third Reich.

This would most certainly stir those S.S. formations in Maribor to frantic endeavour; even now the regular military forces would be flying like angry hornets from the nest. By now truck loads of well armed German infantry would be speeding along the roads in our direction either to winkle us out directly or to block our further passage to the south when we moved as move we must.

My thinking was quickly confirmed by the Partisan commander and before half of our troops had finished their soup, we were on the move again, straight up the next ridge and down the other side but all the time getting into higher and tougher country.

By nightfall we were in well wooded hills to the north west of Sloven Bistrica. I am not certain whether our stopping place was a tiny village or a large farmstead. It was in any case a Partisan rendezvous for here were five Partisans with the nine British prisoners of war from the farming camp of which I had informed the commander the previous night. As it happened, the raiding party had mistaken the directions I gave them and liberated a nearby camp of 10 French prisoners of war first. Naturally they brought them along too. Now we were an international brigade:

Here too, the Partisans inducted a number of reinforcements from the locality among whom I recognised a couple of Maribor civilians. At this time they seemed to have enough rifles and ammunition in store with which to equip the intake. Be it said the rifles captured that morning were soon re issued. Uniforms they did not have so that new recruits had to be content to wear a red star on whatever headgear they brought with them until such time as they could capture an outfit from the enemy.

One of the civilians from Maribor was a man of about forty years of age. After he had received his rifle he came to me, obviously in very real distress. He was in business in the city and, as a good Slovene but nevertheless a wise one, he had done his best to avoid any direct entanglement with the Germans. However, for the last year or so for some reason not clear, the *Gestapo* had been paying him and his family quite a deal of attention. His home and premises had been searched on three occasions and a couple of days before he had been tipped off that he was likely to be arrested any day. On receiving this information he had driven out into the hills in the truck belonging to his business to take refuge with a farmer friend. In due course he was directed to the Partisans who had promptly accepted him, as a Slovene, into their ranks.

Now he bitterly regretted having left his wife and two daughters whose photo he showed me. If he had remained, the *Gestapo* may have taken him but they would conceivably have left his family alone. Now his loved ones would be taken as hostages in his stead with probable results that were quite unspeakable.

His distress was so deep and genuine, his fears so utterly well grounded that I, or anyone with a heart for that matter, must have sympathised with him in his plight. I offered him such words of comfort as I could. What could one say in such a situation except that our troubles usually turn out not so badly as we fear in the long run. Keep hoping for the best.

*The site of the raid by the Partisans near Ozhbalt 31 August 1944.
Picture taken from across Drava River.
Note railwayman's cottage in centre of picture.*

1985
L to R:

Les Laws	*Ivan Kovachic*	*The Author*	*Ferents*
	Former Partisan		*Former Partisan*
	Company Commander		

The two former partisans took part in the raid at Ozhbalt.

Page 56

Apparently my powers of persuasion were inadequate. A quarter of an hour later he stuck the muzzle of his rifle in his mouth and pulled the trigger.

That incident ended quite a day for me. I stretched out on a grassy bank and slept the sleep of exhaustion.

Morning came all too soon so far as sufficiency of sleep was concerned.

On the other hand the majority of my fellows, scantily clad as they were, had almost frozen during the night and looked to the sun rise as the only hope of thawing out. Breakfast consisted of a hot gruel, the main ingredients of which were maize meal and potatoes, not the most exciting repast with which to start the day but nevertheless not to be despised under the circumstances. If the Partisans could campaign on it, I was prepared to accept that we could march on it - there were no alternatives.

Of one thing I was sure: I would not have won a popularity poll right then among some of my own men; the Frenchmen made it obvious that they wished me to hell and beyond. Although they were much better clothed than most of us, they complained from the moment I met them and scarcely let up until we finally parted company some three weeks later.

In the event I had no time to listen. With daylight, those German spotter planes would be out and about again and we were still far too close to their base at Maribor for any degree of comfort at all.

The Partisan commander was of like mind and by seven o'clock the whole column of some 200 men was again on the march. The Partisans were obviously expert in reconnaissance and kept themselves well informed of the Germans' whereabouts. It was doubtless because of this knowledge that we now headed westwards into the well wooded mountain country away from main roads and from habitation generally.

At all times there were parties of two or three Partisans a few kilometres in front of us or a similar distance on our flanks. From time to time one of their number would come back to the column to report. I recall fording several sizeable mountain streams and crossing one quite respectable macadam road. Most of the time we were marching up and down well timbered slopes and although the going was difficult, we were grateful for the cover because, as anticipated, there was soon a German "reccy" aircraft droning overhead. By midday we had probably made eight miles or so. Everything seemed to be going according to whatever plans the Partisans had in mind.

Chapter Five
Ambushed!

A nd now a surprising development came up. It was here on a lovely wooded hillside that we came up with another detachment of guerillas. This body appeared to be about 100 strong and was therefore probably considered a battalion. As I was to learn many years later, they were part of the famous Latsko Detachment named after a Slovene leader and patriot who had been martyred by the Germans some three years earlier. This band consisted of locals operating in their own home locality.

Clenched fist salutes were exchanged and the troops of each detachment mingled together to exchange the latest news. Counting the two Partisan formations together with the thirty or so recruits and the hundred odd allied escapees there must have been nigh on three hundred and fifty men or, more correctly, people gathered together in that piece of woodland. I was told that we would be remaining here until nightfall. The first Partisan detachment handed over the recruits, our former prison guards and the five civilian railway workers to the local "battalion". Coming from an area so close to the Austrian border quite a number of troops of the Latsko detachment could speak reasonably good German. A good looking eighteen year old whom I was to remember for the next twenty seven years as Franchek was assigned to me as interpreter and for the next eight days he practically never left my side. His first piece of information for me was that our original liberators would be leaving us in half an hour or so and shortly thereafter I was shaking hands with the two young lieutenants and wishing them good luck and goodbye. I lined our party up and we gave the men of the battalion three extremely hearty cheers as they marched away out of our lives. Shortly thereafter Franchek introduced me to a dour and taciturn young man who with a party of nine Partisans would lead us on our further journey. So spare of speech was he that it was twenty seven years on before I learned his proper name. May I explain here that no Partisan fought under his proper name; all names were "noms de guerre". Thus even under torture if captured, they could not betray the identity of their comrades in arms and thus bring German retribution down on the heads of the latters' families. Our leader's cover name was, ironically, Sveik.[6] He had the rank of company Commissar which of course meant that political indoctrination of the troops was his principal mission in life.

Shortly thereafter the main body of the Latsko Detachment marched off with the recruits leaving us with our Partisan escort now reduced to ten men. By this time our former guards had been forced to exchange clothing with the more poorly dressed Partisans.

As the sun set we made ready to move on having been informed that, in the normal course of events, most of our marching would be done at night. As we were about to get under way I saw that we were leaving the Austrians, guards and civilians where they were. Franchek confirmed that they were being turned loose to find their way as best they could back to Maribor. I shook hands with them all and wished them good luck. I learnt some months afterwards that they made it back to Maribor in two days apparently none the worse for the untoward happenings which had overtaken them.

Our party, as dusk turned to darkness, moved out of the woodland down the hillside and marched along a well defined track leading gently up the valley. Soon the moon rose which helped to make the going more comfortable. Marching by night and resting by day was highly acceptable to my men as the exercise of marching would keep them warm during the chill of the night and sleep would become at least a feasible proposition during the warmth of the day. As dawn was breaking we came to a large farmstead where a most welcome hot breakfast was waiting for us. Even though it was pretty humble fare most of the way I never ceased to marvel at the way those Slovene peasants managed to keep the food up to their Partisans while at the same time clearly proving to the Germans that they had nothing more than the minimum necessary for subsistence.

Bidding my party to stay within hail I went off the confer with the leader. He was as ever niggardly with his words and very aloof; I could not help wondering if, perhaps, he felt that such close association with so many scions of capitalism might tarnish the purity of his Marxist credo. During the whole of our association we never really did conduct a proper conversation and confined ourselves to the exchange of purely essential information. Anyway, ideologies at this stage were not my worry. If he succeeded in guiding us to safety, I should be only too happy to confirm his wisdom in cleaving to whatever political philosophy appealed to him.

Right now it was obvious that we must confer in order to establish what the immediate plans were. I therefore settled down with Sveik and Franchek, the interpreter, to study a proper ordnance map; it appeared that we were about seven miles south west of Slovenj Gradec. Our future movement, Sveik told me, would naturally depend on circumstances. While we could not expect to avoid German patrols altogether, the idea was to avoid any real collision with them. Rarely would we be further than ten miles from the nearest German forces and often, such as when we had to cross roads and railways, we could be within a couple of hundred yards of enemy elements.

In view of this latter situation I was to divide my men into sections of ten or so each under a recognised leader; by this means we would be able to take the riskier hazards in bounds, a section at a time.

Partisan forces in the course of normal operations would be screening our march to a greater or lesser extent most of the time.

I returned to my party and again divided the men into sections and appointed leaders for them. I then dismissed them with the advice that they had better get some sleep while they could. They needed no second bidding and soon they had disposed themselves in the barns, stalls and hayricks of the farmstead to take full advantage of the warm sunshine which now spread over this most beautiful countryside. I certainly had no trouble getting off to sleep and so soundly did I rest that it was well into the afternoon before I woke. Franchek beside me woke at the same time as I did and we got up and moved toward the farmhouse to see if there was anything new afoot. Before we reached the farmhouse, however, quite a surprise was in store for us. There, sitting on a log was a chunky young-ish civilian, bootless and dressed only in shorts and shirt with his hands firmly tied behind his back and roped to the log on which he was sitting. One of the Partisans was standing guard over him. It seemed he was a Slovene who had been caught spying for the Germans. The Partisans had somehow or another lured him from Maribor out into the mountains and taken him prisoner. He had been delivered to our party a couple of hours previously and was to accompany us on our march to the so called safer areas in the south. I felt at the time that our ten guides had enough on their hands piloting a hundred plus unarmed men through their heavily occupied homeland without the additional responsibility of escort-ing a highly dangerous traitor.

The prisoner was pudgy faced and altogether a rather unattractive looking young man. He certainly did not give the appearance of suffering from malnutrition. I don't know whether he thought I looked more tender hearted than his captors but he implored me to intercede for him explaining that it was all a misunderstanding and that there could not be a more loyal Slovene than he was. I told him that his situation was purely a domestic matter and none of my business. He had best reserve his defensive persuasions for the investigation to which his countrymen planned to subject him at a later date.

In any event it was time to move off again.

Our escort secured their prisoner by keeping his hands bound behind his back and running a rope round his waist which was then secured to the belt of one of their number. With this detail attended to we moved off in our sections in the gathering dusk. We kept going steadily by moonlight along steep valleys between towering mountains. Pausing at daybreak we made a quick breakfast of wholemeal bread, sustaining even if not exciting fare. We marched on for perhaps a further hour which brought us to another farmstead where we were made welcome.

At that time all we wanted was sleep and we quickly disposed ourselves in the ricks and barns. I seemed scarcely to have dozed off when I was wakened by an agitated Franchek with the news that our dangerous prisoner had given us the slip and was now doubtless on his way to the nearest German headquarters with information as to our whereabouts. Sloven Gradec a good sized market town known to be garrisoned by the Germans was little more than fifteen miles away.

Just how the wretched young man had succeeded in slipping his bonds and eluding our escort no one seemed to know. In any event there was no time for explanations or recriminations. It was already mid afternoon we must get going with all speed.

We moved off in our sections and shortly came to a tumbledown shed where we found a couple of Partisans with a meal prepared for us. It had been prepared for later in the day but we were in no position to wait. Again it was a hot vegetable stew with a suggestion of meat in it but it was accepted with relish by us all. Incidentally it was interesting to notice the number of our men who had already managed to scrounge a vessel of some sort from which to eat - old cans, discarded cups or pannikins, glass jars - anything served so long as it was hollow.

The meal finished, we were on our way again this time following a well defined track which took us through more open country. Even with our depleted escort there were always three of our guides either out ahead or scouting our flanks as a guard against surprise. A fine looking Partisan known as Cholo, was permanent forward scout. He was a regular soldier in the old Jugoslav army and had "taken to the woods" on the collapse of Jugoslav resistance in April 1941. He seemed tireless. He certainly served us well. From time to time - the word would be passed to keep absolute silence while we marched - no talking and careful footsteps. Somewhere early in this evening we crossed a macadam road that obviously carried substantial traffic. We crossed this a section at a time with two of the Partisans some couple of hundred yards along the road on either side of our crossing.

Whether such care was necessary on that occasion I do not know, but the exercise served as good practice for the many later occasions when utmost caution had to be observed. By later standards it was an uneventful night and daybreak found us safely in timbered hill country again ready to rest up for the day. Shortly after our arrival a couple of large pots of unknown origin arrived containing the ration of maize and potato porridge for breakfast. A stack of round loaves of black bread which we cut into wedges and a small sack of apples were also on hand in the same magical fashion to ensure that we would have something to keep us going in the middle of the day.

From this and other signs it was obvious that we were now reaching the Slovenian heartland where civilian support for the Partisans was almost total. This ensured that we would be kept well informed of German troop movements and strong points but did not alter the fact that the enemy with tanks, armoured cars, artillery and air support could still bring an overwhelming superiority of arms to bear on the Partisans (and us) should it perchance come to a direct confrontation in daylight; hence we had to be ready to move at any time on a couple of minutes notice.

During that same afternoon while we were sleeping or merely resting up a scout came in to report. Immediately I heard the word with which I was to become very familiar over the days ahead "*Gremo*" roughly "Let's get moving." Apparently the Fritz was getting too close for comfort.

Our men were quickly roused and in under five minutes we were moving off.

Evening brought us to a farmstead where again a wash copper of hot stew was awaiting us. The farm overlooked a quite substantial river valley and the hillsides were covered with orchards of apple and pear trees in full bearing, vineyards loaded with grapes almost ready to be vintaged to produce the very good local riesling, and well laden plum trees to provide the raw material for slivovitz, Jugoslavia's special plum brandy.

It was a countryside of surpassing beauty and I could not but recall the line, "where every prospect pleases and only man is vile".

The farmer and his family were naturally curious at the arrival of so large a body of Angleski or Englander, their language switching with complete facility from Slovene to Austrian German depending on the audience. This bilingualism was (and still is) widely prevalent in Slovenia particularly in the north.

Our guide and I spent a half hour or so with the farmer and his wife in the kitchen while the troops finished their evening meal. The young commissar, ever eager to propagate "the faith", delivered them a brief lecture on the glories of the communist cause to which they listened politely if unenthusiastically. As the kitchen was adorned with the usual quota of holy pictures and the corner shrine usually found in older style Roman Catholic homes, the lack of audience response was scarcely surprising.

The farmer appeared to take the line that, in spite of all dangers, he would gladly assist the Partisans with every resource he had to throw out the Germans but if they were only going to get Russians by way of exchange, then it was all just a waste of life and effort. What was needed, he seemed to be saying, was a loosely federated Jugoslavia with the accent on local autonomy. Slovenes had always got along with their Austrian and Italian neighbours; they had a beautiful land easily capable of feeding its population; they never had and never would offer a threat to anyone else. Why couldn't foreigners generally leave them in peace to work and live according to the faith of their fathers handed down over a thousand years.

Our young guide shook his head sadly at such a demonstration of petit bourgeois thinking but recalled in time that his present assignment was a military one and that dialectics would have to wait. Sometime that night we would have to ford a small stream and cross a well used road. This would tend to slow us down so once again it was "*Gremo*". The farmer kindly provided us with two sides of mutton by way of provisions. These were lashed to stakes to make them more easily portable by teams of two.

We marched along the hillside through the orchards and then down the slope to the river bank a couple of miles upstream. The stream at this point was perhaps 25 feet wide and flowing strongly, purling and gurgling over a rocky bed. The ford by which we crossed was built up with heavy boulders filled in with smaller stones. It was obviously constructed to carry farm carts and wagons; motorised vehicles would need to take it in low gear. As it was, the water was some inches deep. Inches deep water flowing strongly over slippery stones calls for careful stepping on the part of a pedestrian. Fortunately the entire party made it safely with only a half dozen or so of us getting a full length bath. Even so these were snow fed waters and I found it distinctly uncomfortable.

We pressed on along a farm track once more through open fields in bright moonlight. We had perhaps made another five miles; I could make out the dim outline of some buildings about four hundred yards ahead probably another farm house. I was up at the head of the column with Sveik and Franchek. Cholo was, as usual, well out in front. He took a flashlight from his pack and flashed it on and off a few times in the direction of the house. Obviously he was signalling to the occupants. There was no answer. He repeated the process. Still no answer. There was a hurried consultation and two of the Partisans were ordered forward to investigate.

Suddenly out of the night came the challenge "*Wer da!*" This was trouble - real trouble: that call was unmistakable German for "who goes there" shouted in equally unmistakable German accents. Our escaped spy had executed his traitorous mission with speed and efficiency. Without a word from me, or anyone else, a hundred bodies hit the ground as one. Again the challenge "*Wer da!*" This time the challenge was answered "Partisan".

I suppose those Germans knew they were on foreign soil where nobody loved them. They were probably only a small detachment. They had no doubt become pretty nervous sitting there in the dark waiting for they knew not what. At all events on the reply to their challenge a truly tremulous yell came from the farm house "*PAAARRTISAN*" and, on the instant, a prolonged rattle of medium machine gun fire. The Partisans replied with Sten gun and rifle the former for sound effect only as the range was too great. The firing broke off for a couple of seconds long enough for Sveik to shout at the top of his voice in best parade ground style "Partisan battalion! *naprej!*" (advance). Whether the Germans understood the actual command or not was beside the point; they could not misunderstand that they were being confronted by a battalion of merciless brigands from whom not the faintest suggestion of quarter could be expected.

They opened up again with everything they had. Now the danger to us was probably only slight; the enemy couldn't see us, and as we had gone to ground we were in any case a poor target. Five of our Partisans had moved well away from the track and were drawing the enemy fire to the flashes of their Stens and rifles. It is all very well, however, to consider this in the cold light of hindsight. What mattered was that we were a hundred unarmed men who had seen neither drill, bivouac, exercises, manoeuvres much less genuine battle conditions in three years. The rattle of the machine guns, the whistle of bullets overhead was too much. Franchek shouted in German "Go back.' Run" Our men could understand that much German and complied on the instant. Franchek scrambled to his feet catching me a nasty blow in the right eye with his boot heel as he did so and almost winding me with his first step by getting his foot in my back as he sprang past me.

The Commissar commander shouted to his men to continue the action for the moment and signalled to me to get back to my troops and regroup them in some woodland a quarter of a mile or so down the track on the left. The troops unfortunately had not waited on any orders and were already in full flight. I bellowed for all I was worth "Don't run don't scatter" Apparently in my semi winded condition I did not get enough volume behind the "don'ts" as the rearward sections, now leading the stampede later claimed that they could only hear me calling "Run scatter", which demonstrates the necessity of keeping directives positive.

By the time Sveik and I reached the timber we were practically leaders without a following. A quick count of heads only made up a dozen or so. For a few minutes it looked as if my soaring ambitions had crashed at the first hurdle. Should we maintain silence? Should we move? What the blazes should we do?

Bidding the few fellows to stay put I moved off into the trees whistling and calling out softly "anyone about?" "Come on men" and similar obvious nonsense. I rounded up about another ten including two who had faithfully hung on to their side of mutton. I had just rejoined my original party which at least now contained all the original escapees when salvation appeared in the bulky form of Don Funston, a husky Victorian from East Preston.

September 1944
"Cholo" leading "Sveik", "Franchek", The Author, Les Laws and Company

Don was a practical young man; finesse was probably not his greatest attribute. He opined that we couldn't stand around here all bloody night, nor would it be smart to have some seventy of our men straggling about all over the bloody countryside for Jerry to pick up piecemeal. The few Fritzes back there were probably in just as big a panic as we were. The more bloody noise we made the better - give the Hun the idea that we were mounting a battalion attack. With that he started to bellow in a voice that the Stentor couldn't have matched even with a loud hailer.

He informed all interested listeners within the surrounding half mile that the main party was forming up and would be moving off in five minutes. Any stragglers who didn't want to be left behind had better join us at the bloody double. Direct and very effective. They came from the woods, they crawled out of the adjoining fields and by the time we had reformed our sections only four of our men were missing. I regretted particularly that among those missing were Bert Avis and Reg Allen, old hands from the St. Egidi road building days. The other side of mutton was also missing having been ditched in the panic.

Our leader was now obviously uncertain. The farmhouse we had approached was a Partisan staging point where he had hoped to pick up information as to the whereabouts of both Germans and Partisans. He informed me briefly that we would have a long march in front of us to the next "safe" area, that we would have to keep going all night and probably well into the next day as well.

Without our noticing it, Cholo had already started a detour; together with another two of our escort, he had called at a neighbouring farmhouse and "conscripted" the farmer's seventeen year old son to act as our local guide. He and his party met us as we emerged from the trees on the far side of the woodland.

We then set off at a brisk step and kept going without a rest for some three hours. Somewhere about three in the morning one of the tireless scouts reported in. Let me here pay tribute to these men. How fit they must have been covering as they did at least two miles for every mile we made. They were utterly fearless, operating on their own, armed only with a Sten gun or a rifle.

On this occasion there was information that a courier was waiting for us at a farmhouse a bit further along the way. In half an hour we were there to receive the welcome news that the Partisans had created a major diversion back towards Celje and that we were comparatively safe where we were. Where we were, by then, according to the guide's large scale map was in steep hill country a few miles north of the township of Mozirje.

The farmstead was happily blessed with numerous hay ricks, hay lofts and sheds. All hands settled down thankfully for a sleep in reasonable comfort, at least the best they had had since the break out.

CHAPTER SIX
PRECIS OF PARTISAN HISTORY

Although it creates a digression from the main narrative it is probably appropriate at this point to tell something of the Partisans history and grand strategy as I was now coming to know it from conversations with Franchek and others.

The movement had its beginnings in mid 1941 immediately following the German invasion of Jugoslavia in April. At that time Josip Broz had been Secretary General of the underground Jugoslav Communist party for some years. Tito was one of the numerous *"noms de guerre"* he had used during those years as a cover from the Royal Jugoslav authorities according to whose laws the Communist party was a seditious organisation to be completely exterminated, root and branch. The Royal Jugoslav Government in exile in the early months recognised only Mihailovitch and his *Chetniks* in south eastern Serbia as an official resistance movement. Tito and his communist organisation they totally ignored.

The great allies at that time fighting the Germans, Britain and Russia, both officially recognised the Royal Jugoslav Government in exile as representing the Jugoslav nation, and, having official diplomatic representation with them, adopted the same attitude. In the early days of the occupation the Germans also took the same line.

In any event the Germans, assisted or perhaps hindered by their Italian, Hungarian and Bulgarian allies had completely shattered the ramshackle Jugoslav military machine and partitioned the country by way of annexing certain territories to themselves, setting up a nominally independent puppet state in Croatia and leaving the remainder under nominal local quisling governments closely supervised by the occupying military forces in much the same way as they had done in France, and Norway. In June 1941 the Germans invaded Russia.

By that time they were confident that Jugoslavia would pose no problems. After all it was a poor country populated in the main by a poor and backward people who had no coherent history as a nation to hold them together. If an ancient, populous and cultured nation such as France with its great martial and cultural traditions going back well over a thousand years could be brought to accept the German jackboot firmly pressed in the middle of its back, what was there to worry about from fifteen, sixteen million Slav "*Untermenschen*" lacking culture, tradition, a sense of national unity and above all the physical means of mounting any sort of action worthy of the name of resistance.

Accordingly by the end of June 1941 the Germans and their allies withdrew their front line troops from Jugoslavia to tackle the more earnest business of active warfare on the various fighting fronts, most particularly in Russia and also in North Africa. The newly conquered land of the South Slavs they left to the care of second line garrison troops and the armies of the various puppet states and quisling governments.

To Josip Broz Tito and his communist party, the German occupation made little difference. They had been working underground against authority for years. They had a very efficient secret communications network covering most of the country and this was now used to set up the organisation of a national army of resistance.

By the beginning of August 1941 both Partisans and *Chetniks* operating independently of each other were seriously harassing the Axis occupation forces and disrupting their lines of communication. The *Chetniks* at least were reasonably equipped with the Jugoslav military small arms with which they had retreated to their mountain fastnesses before the German juggernaut five months before. The Partisans, on the other hand, had, in the main, only a miscellany of sporting rifles, shot guns and such equipment as they could acquire in the process of wiping out small isolated enemy garrisons by sheer weight of numbers.

The independent operations of the two separate movements were in any case sufficient to convince the Axis that its original assumption of torpid quiescence on the part of the Jugoslavs was not only premature but also dangerously fallacious. The garrison troops were hastily reinforced with ill spared front line divisions supported by elements of the elite arms, the S.S. and the S.D. The most savage reprisals were taken on the civilian population - public executions by the hundreds, destruction of villages, removal of men by the thousands to Germany as slave labour and so on.

Tito and Mihailovitch did actually meet in conference on a couple of occasions but the gap between their respective communist and royalist ideologies, their backgrounds and above all their differing concepts of objective strategy was too wide to be bridged.

The directions of the Government in exile served only to confound the confusion. Broadcasting from London over the BBC they ordered by turns that the population accept the occupation without resistance because of the inevitable waste of human life and property that would otherwise ensue. Then they directed that all resistance had to be commanded and controlled by Mihailovitch whom they promoted from Colonel to General to enhance his prestige. The communists were either to be won over or exterminated. This latter was too much for the British and, of course, the Russians and was quickly countermanded publicly. Secretly, however, Mihailovitch was instructed by his Government-in-exile to regard the Partisans as being more dangerous to Jugoslavia than were the occupying Axis forces.

By the winter of 1941/42 Tito and his Partisans therefore found themselves contending not only with the Germans and the Italians but also with their own countrymen. This was probably the nadir of Tito's fortunes comparable with Washington's Valley Forge. He had no means of communicating with the outside world. Mihailovitch was at least in radio contact with his Government through Cairo. Such damage as was inflicted on the occupying forces by the Partisans was automatically credited to the *Chetniks*. So much was this the case that a British officer was dropped into Mihailovitch by parachute followed somewhat later by a full scale military mission and soon a steady supply of British arms and ammunition was being dropped into the *Chetniks*, who used them against the Partisans rather than against the Germans.

Incredibly, throughout most of 1942 Tito remained almost unrecognised and unknown among the Great Allies. Such shadowy information as came out of Europe concerning him was largely via German media. This was predictably false and unflattering.

The name Tito was at first believed to apply to a committee rather than an individual. The Partisans were represented as being nothing more than roving bands of brigands taking advantage of their country's unhappy plight to murder, rape and plunder. That they were in any way a recognisable coherent military organisation was well over a year in gaining acceptance outside Jugoslavia.

The Germans of course were well aware of the truth. By the spring of 1942, Mihailovitch had reached a secret accord with Neditch the Serbian puppet Prime Minister whereby the *Chetniks* would cease their campaign of destruction and restrict their attacks on German garrisons to a level just sufficient to hoodwink the few British officers in their midst. Thus would German reprisals against civilian populations be largely reduced if not altogether avoided. The Germans in turn were able to turn all their attention to rooting out the Partisans in their principal strongholds in Bosnia Herzegovina leaving the *Chetniks*, supplied with British arms, to attend to the security of Serbia. A typically "Balkan" situation, albeit a macabre and tragic one.

Josip Broz was a dedicated communist but a dedicated communist with a significant and contradictory difference. He was a Jugoslav nationalist to the core. He believed in the right of well defined ethnic groups to run their own affairs without external interference as passionately as ever Woodrow Wilson did. He believed that the Jugoslavia created at Versailles in 1919 could, if properly constituted, become a viable nation. In short he represented in one person for Jugoslavia, what the triumvirate of Mazzini, Cavour and Garibaldi had represented for Italy eighty odd years earlier.

In one respect he was the complete communist and that was in his total disregard for the cost in human life and property of achieving his aims. There was no price he would not pay, no sacrifice he would not make, to oust the invader from Jugoslavia. Help he would accept, accept it gladly no matter whence it came, so long as it came with no strings attached. Post war Jugoslavia had to be free and uncommitted.

A so to say National Communist, he had gathered about him in his illegal days in the late thirties an academic elite made up of members of many aristocratic and middle class Jugoslav families who had both the perception and patriotism to accept the fact that the Kingdom of the South Slavs based as it was on Serbian hegemony, could not last.

In those grim winter weeks of 1941/2 the grand strategy was formulated. The most mountainous, rough and broken areas would be held by the Partisans. These were areas where the enemy would find it impossible to use his tanks and heavy artillery. Concealed from view in craggy or wooded ravines the Partisans would have little to fear from the enemy's air power. To send in infantry against them the enemy would first have to locate them. The Partisans with their superior knowledge of the terrain would be able to inflict severe casualties on opposing foot soldiers. Supposing the latter were too strong numerically to be halted, the lightly equipped Partisans could always retire to the next redoubt and inflict further casualties on the advancing enemy until he was halted or forced by sheer attrition to withdraw.

The central control would be flexible at all times. Each band would operate in its own home area so as to capitalise to the fullest on the advantage of local knowledge. These bands or companies would be led by thoroughly trained professional officers. A comprehensive intelligence network would be set up in all the major towns and cities based on the existing communist underground to keep the Partisans informed of all major enemy activity. Communication would be by courier, intrepid youths of fifteen and even younger.

The objectives were simple: to destroy the enemy and his lines of communication by lightning raids on his garrisons and convoys, on the roads, railways, bridges and viaducts or anything else that

1977 Maribor
"Cholo" Karel Cholnik,   Ronte   The Author "Franchek" Franjo Vesenjak

1972 Maribor
"Sveik" France Gruden   The Author   "Franchek" Franjo Vesenjak

could harass or hinder his operations. No attempt was to be made to hold fixed positions except the inaccessible mountain redoubts already described.

To ensure maximum support from the widest possible spread of the civilian population, the communist foundations of the movement were played down. The governing body was called the National Anti Fascist Council and the official style of the Partisans was the National Army of Liberation.

By the late summer of 1942 this organisation and strategy had already achieved quite remarkable results out of all proportion to the men and materiel that the Partisans were able to bring to bear. The infuriated Germans found themselves deploying division after division of precious front line troops including paratroops and S.S. in an attempt to destroy an enemy who was doing them most grievous bodily harm but who could not be brought to battle. When this failed they concentrated every military resource at their command on guarding every mile of road and railway, every bridge and every viaduct against the depredations of the accursed Partisans. Nowhere in their conquered territories had they encountered anything like it. Nowhere in their military manuals was there a suggestion of successful counter measures. By the time Britain, the first of the Great Allies to appreciate the situation, dropped a military mission into Tito in the early summer of 1943 the Partisans were already in practical and undisputed possession of quite sizeable areas of Bosnia, Dalmatia and Slovenia where the rugged terrain gave them so many advantages. The Italians had long since abandoned the attempt to keep up even an appearance of coping; the Partisans regarded Italian garrisons as their easiest and most valuable source of arms and ammunition.

The Germans, made of sterner stuff, continued to hold the larger towns and cities, the broad river valleys and the plains but largely abandoned the highlands to an enemy, the pursuit of whom was too costly in troops and whose defeat when brought to battle was in any case indecisive owing to his ability to disengage and withdraw in good order whenever it suited him.

True the Germans launched numerous direct offensives on Tito's personal headquarters. They offered an enormous reward in gold for his capture dead or alive. Several times he escaped his pursuers by the narrowest of margins leaving the infuriated Hun to vent his spleen on every hapless civilian in the locality.

True also, the Partisans suffered unbelievably severe casualties. Limited as their arms were, their medical services were even thinner. Apart from Germans and Italians they had to contend with Serbian *Chetniks*, Croatian Ustasha and Slovenian Bela Garde. For the Ustasha and Bela Garde the Partisans reserved a special ferocious hatred. These were not only fascists, they were traitors as well. For them on the morrow of victory there could be no forgiveness; to the Partisans they were lower than the meanest reptiles.

This is broadly the story as the Partisans saw it. By the time I joined them in the late summer of 1944 their worst days were over. They were now recognised and supported by all three Great Allies. The Italians had gone, the Germans were pinned down, the local puppets and fascist quislings were already savouring the first doubts of coming out on the right side and most importantly the Partisans were now receiving more recruits than they could immediately arm.

Making allowances for their wild enthusiasm for their cause and their achievements which naturally coloured their view of recent history, even conceding the exaggerations and improperly based assumptions, the record was a heroic one, probably without parallel in modern times.

CHAPTER SEVEN
MARCH TO THE SAVA

By the time we awoke the sun was well up in the sky. There was news that in two separate engagements on the previous day and night sizeable bodies of Partisans had managed to ambush two large bodies of our pursuers and inflict such damage on them as to give them pause to consider whether recapturing a few score prisoners was worth the risk of venturing into the wild country to which the Partisans would surely have led us. It appeared that severe casualties had been inflicted on the enemy. In addition to destroying a number of vehicles, the Partisans had also captured intact an armoured car, a truck, a medium gun and a useful collection of small arms and ammunition. This was apparently a most exciting result.

Our taciturn guide, Sveik then informed me laconically that this was the reason why the young lieutenant brigadier had been so enthusiastic about liberating the whole of our team instead of settling for the original seven. He had correctly judged that whereas the Germans might well have taken no special measures to pursue the smaller party, they would almost certainly give chase to the larger one. After all, our camp in Maribor was quite prominently sited and well known. Our escape could scarcely be concealed from the civilians. It would never do to let the locals believe for a moment that German security was so ineffective.

The company of Partisans we had encountered at Lovrenc were only part of a total formation of almost a thousand who had been holed up in the hills waiting upon whatever moves the Germans might make. The raid on Lovrenc was itself designed to stir the Germans up. Our fortuitous arrival on the scene had been accepted as the final catalyst necessary to ensure the appropriate reaction. The original liberation took place at 8.00 am Thursday, 31st August. An hour later the air raid sirens of Maribor sounded: every P.O.W. in the area was evacuated to Austria proper on a half hour's notice.

So we had been used as bait, used very successfully. Our allies and liberators certainly didn't miss many tricks. As a result of all this the area in which we now found ourselves could be considered "safe". "Safe" in this particular context was strictly a relative expression only. We were now only thirty to thirty five miles away from Ljubljana, the capital of Slovenia. This ancient city, was at that time, a vital communications centre for the Germans. There the railway from Vienna Maribor made a junction with the line from Villach to the north west which linked up with the lines in southern Germany. Owing to the great attention which the Allied Air forces had been paying the more direct line through the Brenner pass, these alternative railways were vital to the Germans for supplying Kesselring's armies in Italy as well reinforcing the troops trying to contain the Partisans in Dalmatia and southern Slovenia.

Apart from railways, Ljubljana was also the centre of a whole complex of highways and lesser roads equally important to the German lines of communication. The city and its immediate environs were therefore strongly garrisoned by the Germans and the local quisling *Bela Garde* (White Guards) and no place for ninety odd unarmed prisoners of war on the run, even though its Slovene civilian population was in the main strongly pro Partisan.

We had now been at large for four days and, apart from the brief encounter a few hours before, had had a trouble free passage. However, the young commissar now pointed out to me that the country we had crossed thus far had been easy because it was of no real strategic significance to the enemy and therefore only thinly occupied by him. The country we were approaching and through which we would have to march for the next few days was different, very different. We would be in country crisscrossed by roads and railways of such strategic importance that the whole area would be heavily garrisoned and patrolled by German forces. Our further journey would be by circuitous routes, decided upon from day to day as the military situation dictated.

My most tactful enquiries failed to elicit our ultimate destination in Jugoslavia or the means whereby we were eventually to find ourselves safely behind the Allied lines if indeed this were the intention. Either our taciturn guide did not know himself or deemed it unwise for security reasons to inform me.

As noted earlier in this narrative, not all of our party were willing participants; some were quite frank with their objections. POW camp life with all its restrictions, deprivations and rough living was, at least, as safe a place to be as anywhere in Europe. If Laws and I were about seeking honour and glory, bully for us; but why did we have to involve them. Here they were being marched through enemy territory by a few lightly armed peasants without any arms of their own for self defence - this against well armed and trained German soldiers with artillery, armour and aircraft to support them. We had lost four good mates the night before; how many more would we lose before we got to wherever we were supposed to be going? How did we propose to get them out of the country anyway? Let me say at once that these dissenters were very much a minority but, nevertheless, sufficiently numerous as to be a threat to morale.

I therefore took the opportunity of addressing the entire party and putting to them our position as I saw it. I told them that there were British troops, - officers and other ranks, operating with the Partisans at no great distance from where we were now resting. We had equally as good a chance of survival as they did. We had not pulled on uniforms to be Hitler's guests. We were British soldiers with a clear duty to fight the enemy with everything at our disposal. Were they really happy to go on bludging on the hard-rationed folks at home who had supported us through the Red Cross so magnificently over the last three years? Laws and I in organising their release, had sought to do nothing more than give them a chance to get back to their loved ones earlier than they could have hoped and get on with the duty they had solemnly sworn do.

Those who so wished could, so far as I was concerned, break off right away and return to captivity - I had no authority to stop them. They should bear in mind, however, that, in doing so, they would become, technically at least, deserters. Furthermore they should remember that they had taken part in an action in which German soldiers had been disarmed and captured - mutiny; they might have some trouble convincing a German court-marshal that they had not been willing participants. Les Laws conveyed the gist of my message to the Frenchmen. My words certainly muted the outright protests even if a few mumbles and grumbles persisted.

Not that I expected my admonition to work an immediate miracle; the toughest troops in the world would be unlikely to stand up to any semblance of battle conditions after three years' absence from the training and indoctrination of barrack room and bivouac. I could only hope for the best.

As a measure for better control I arranged with Sveik that I would move along the line of marchers from time to time instead of remaining with him constantly. Should he wish to communicate with me he could send Franchek to me. This, I believed, would give all hands a feeling of coherence; furthermore, I arranged to change the order of march with a different section leading after every halt.

These changes were probably worthwhile because, although we did not have further collisions with the enemy like the previous night's skirmish, we did have a number of near encounters which might otherwise have caused panic and further loss of numbers.

We spent the whole of that day resting; whether this was dictated by the military situation or whether it was a matter of resting us after so many days of unaccustomed foot slogging I was unable to establish. Possibly both considerations were involved.

It was, I remember, a beautiful day and most of us were happy to catch some extra sleep. We all had to remain within easy call but we happily accepted the consignment of apples and plums which arrived while we were there.

The young man who had been "conscripted" as local guide had, by now, been sent home but had been replaced by another who was familiar with the area over which we would make our next bound. It was obvious from where we stood that we were at the end of the high country on the well-wooded slopes of which we had enjoyed good cover from sight. Our next move would take us into more open undulating country where cover would be much sparser. Patrolled roads and railways would have to be negotiated several times daily, or, rather nightly.

In the event we moved out that night across fields and along roads which were not, apparently of sufficient strategic importance to justify any patrolling, mechanised or otherwise. Nevertheless we were instructed to maintain maximum possible silence and talk, if at all, only in whispers. We kept as far away from any habitation as possible - all houses were likely to have a dog and dogs are kept to alert their masters to intruders by barking. Thus our passing was almost ghostly quiet.

For three nights we marched uneventfully. I seem to recall taking a number of roads patrolled by armoured vehicles in keenly-timed, section by section bounds. There was also, at least one railway which was said to be pill-boxed at intervals of five kilometres with foot patrols moving in between. Naturally the timing for this one was precise.

It should be said here that most of us had, by now grown accustomed to the sound of machine-gun fire at no great distance. Franchek told me to assure my fellows that, far from being alarmed, they should take comfort from the fact that our passage was considered sufficiently important to the Partisans for them to create a diversion on every occasion that we were forced to enter any area where the enemy was present in strength. This was probably the case and there was never a night when our ears did not inform us that machine-gunners were busy. Indeed on several occasions during our fourteen day march we were aroused from our daytime slumber with the urgent call of "*Gremo*" and led quickly away from perceived approaching danger. And usually, from the gunfire not all that far to our rear we were able to assume that our faithful allies were indeed involved in yet another sharp "diversion."

Following the eighth night's march we arrived at a large farmstead just after daybreak where a hot meal was waiting for us. We were told to catch some sleep immediately after the meal as we would be leaving during the course of the afternoon. Sure enough! We were on the move again by two o'clock marching along a well defined dirt road. We could only hope that the Partisans knew what they were doing; I for one felt dreadfully exposed and hoped that all the German reconnaissance aircraft in Slovenia were either grounded or fully engaged elsewhere. We had not gone far when Franchek joined me with the order that we were to form up and march in best parade ground style. We would shortly be parading before some high ranking Partisan officers who would be accompanied by a British officer!

We duly formed up and marched tidily despite the crumpled and grubby uniforms of those of us who had them and the equally grubby "home-made" garb of those who did not. So widely known is the piece that Franchek requested that we sing "Tipperary!' as we marched. By the time we had complied and added 'Pack up Your Troubles" to the repertoire we were within sight of an open field on our right and in it, perhaps a hundred yards from the road was a group of some twenty or thirty people. Our leader turned towards them so I ordered a right wheel; then, as we approached the group a left wheel. By now I could identify several men in British battle dress but I knew that regular air-drops had been coming in to the Partisans for more than a year now and thus, that British uniforms in Slovenia were more likely to be worn by one of Tito's men than by a British soldier. Then I spotted- one of the uniforms with a crown on the epaulettes worn by a well built man probably in his mid to late thirties - a Major no less.

What an occasion! We marched past at 'eyes right" and, the march past completed, came to a halt. We stood easy and I approached the major and saluted him smartly identifying myself at the same time. He raised his hand to return the salute but realised in time that he was without headgear. Instead he reached out his hand and shook mine heartily and, recognising my slouch hat, said with a smile, "You surprise me Corporal[7]. 'I've always understood that Australians reserved their salutes for special people on special occasions." "Believe me, Major," I replied, 'This particular occasion measures up on both counts." Having congratulated me he suggested that we break off so that the escapees could relax and mix with the locals, a few of whom spoke English and even more who spoke German or Italian.

I brought Les over and introduced him as having organised the original get-away. The Major's name, I seem to remember was Jones. I have the feeling he was a Canadian or possibly had lived a long while in our big sister-dominion. There was a certain trans-atlantic style to his speech. While we were chatting we were joined by a shortish Partisan wearing steel rimmed spectacles and a smart enough uniform that was somehow rather more civilian than military. He spoke quite good but halting English and was vastly curious as to our backgrounds. His knowledge of Australia was surprising: he knew that we were a federation, a "democratic kingdom" (his term) which he thought odd and that we presently had a "socialist" government. He had beady dark eyes with which he peered quite intently at his tete-a-tete. I took him to be a school teacher or even, perhaps, a university don.

It turned out that he was the former by profession. This was Edouard Kardelj and, by present occupation, he was Tito's Marxist Dialectician-in-Chief and second only to the Marshal in the Partisan pecking order. He assured us that we were through the worst of it. We had now reached and would continue through areas of little or no strategic interest to the Germans. So long as we co-operated promptly and fully with our escort we should be behind our own lines 'in early time". Well at last it was definite, we were not going to be drafted into the Partisan ranks.

I ventured to ask how we were going to get across the Sava. This was a question that had exercised my mind from the outset. The Sava is the Danube's biggest tributary and a major river by any standards. Naturally it was crossed by a number of bridges and just as naturally every one of those bridges would be heavily guarded with weaponry too heavy for lightly armed guerrillas to tackle. I could not avoid the idea that German Intelligence would have to be very slack if it did not have a pretty good idea of our approximate whereabouts and the direction in which we were heading. Having failed to recapture us early, why not wait for us on a likely stretch of the Sava and take us and our escort as we tried to cross on whatever minor floating transport the Partisans could lay on.

My enquiry was met with a bland but smiling," that, I'm afraid, I cannot tell you. We will wait and see when and where it is safe". My enquiry as to our ultimate exit from Jugoslavia received a simi-larly enigmatic answer. The good Major smiled. "Believe it or not, he probably doesn't know because it probably hasn't been finally decided yet, but these guys are the greatest opportunists and impro-visers you'll ever meet. I'll back them to get you all out somehow. They have an incredible knack of pulling fast ones on 'Fritz' and this operation is enormously important to them prestigewise."

I still look back on this meeting of some one hundred and twenty Allied soldiers on an open meadow in heavily occupied enemy ter-ritory on a sunny September afternoon as one of the most bizarre events in an eighteen day period that was, essentially, a succession of incredibles. The people to whom I spoke all seemed totally relaxed. If they sensed any hint of danger they concealed it completely; and there was no doubt that their attitude had its effect on the pessimists in our party.

I suppose we were there for half an hour or so before forming up again and marching away. At dusk we reached yet another farm and a welcome from the people there. I remember them as a good looking young couple with two pretty children, a girl and a boy both of whom were most curious as to who we were and why we were there. It emerged that they had seen the odd one or two of our RAF pilots, shot down on a mission, arriving for a meal and a rest on their passage south; but ninety nine "Angliski", (actually 91 "British" and 8 French) most of them wearing irregular clothing instead of uniforms, was something outside the youngsters experience. A goodly stew was simmering in the laundry "copper" to which we did full justice. Following the meal we were told to take a short nap as we would have to move on in two hours time.

We were awakened on schedule and marched on through the night, reaching a woodland of sufficient extent to shelter us from sight for the day. This was a testing period: Our only rations for the day consisted of good peasant black bread - not especially appetising but wonderfully sustaining.

Come nightfall and away. Our local guide led us in the usual single file along back roads and across fields as confidently as if he had perfect night vision. First light found us approaching a sizeable area of woodland and into this we marched and continued on for half an hour. Sveik, our escort leader called me over and, through Franchek told me to tell my party to get what rest they could as this day was going to be a very testing one. He then produced a detailed map of the area, a copy of which I subsequently obtained and reproduce here. We were now no more than two kilometres from the Sava at its nearest point and we were to cross it that night. Shortly he would be handing us over to men from another formation and getting us across would be their responsibility. He was a dour but dedicated young man. He was clearly not in good health - his emaciated frame, sallow complexion, and persistent cough suggested TB to me. The onus of guiding our rag-tag band across such country as we had covered, for eight days, always aware of a remorseless enemy, ever ready to strike if opportunity offered, had been a heavy one. Despite his strong reserve I could not help warming to him. Having made sure that sentries were set, he rolled himself up in his blanket for sleep. I did likewise without a blanket but with the advantage of full underwear and sweater under my uniform.

Fortunately, now that we were in lower country, the days were quite warm and all hands were weary enough from marching to get some sleep despite the many cases of inadequate clothing.

CHAPTER EIGHT
ACROSS THE SAVA

I t was midday when I awoke. Doubtless it was the arrival of our new escort that roused me; there were, perhaps, fifteen or twenty of them. Most importantly for the moment, they had brought with them sufficient stew to give us all a good meal; the fact that it was cold in no way stifled our appreciation. How could one beat them!

Their leader was already conferring with Sveik; after the meal Les and I joined them. To our surprise the new man spoke quite good English. He told us that everything was in readiness for our crossing; our principal contribution to its success would be to make as little noise as possible from now on and to make sure that the entire party understood the necessity for absolute silence once the operation was under way. The local farmers had informed the Germans that their horses were needed on the other side of the river where the grain crops were ready for harvest. The Germans accepted this as they knew that there was a deficiency of draught live stock in all occupied areas because they had themselves conscripted so much of it for military purposes. Thus it was quite normal for farming communities to be moving working animals - horses and/or oxen considerable distances from area to area as dictated by seasonal circumstances. As to the necessity for a night time crossing - simple: draught stock were now so scarce that they were needed for a full day's work either side of the river. A night crossing was the only option.[8]

To cover our crossing, the farmers would swim two groups of horses across the Sava that night at points half a kilometre apart commencing at ten o'clock. Assembling the horses and leading them down to the river bank would create quite a degree of confusion and noise. This particular operation would be strung out long enough to cover our approach. While we were being ferried across, the horses would swim over led by riders mounted on horses who were accustomed to it.

Les and I looked at each other and looked again at the map with all its swastika flags. This was going to be indeed a "dicey do". But it had to be done - we just simply had to trust in these incredibly gallant people who were going to such lengths to liberate us.

Sveik now indicated that his party would be leaving us in quarter of an hour to return to the Pohorje.[9] I shook his hand and thanked him for the great service that he and his party had rendered us and wished him and them all a safe return journey.

Apart from Sveik and Franchek I should again mention Cholo, a handsome man who had acted throughout our march as forward scout. He must have been very fit indeed as he ranged anything up to a kilometre in front of us, sometimes alone, sometimes with the local guide ensuring that the "coast was clear". Franchek and I embraced - we had of necessity been almost inseparable for eight days and, not unnaturally, grown very close to each other. He gave me his parents' address and asked me to write to him after the war. The whole party had served us well but it was Sveik, Franchek and Cholo that I remembered and still remember so clearly.

And so they moved out to quiet individual farewells and our sincere good wishes.

While the men were all together in a group I told them of what was planned and what was expected of us. Les and I kept our knowledge of the local map to ourselves. Instead I informed them of what the

Major had told me two days previously concerning the Partisans' ingenuity and his confidence that we would make it safely out of Jugoslavia. In the event everything went so exactly according to plan as to be almost an anti-climax.

As dusk approached we heard the sound of horses being rounded up with much whistling and shouting coming from all directions except that of the river. As soon as it was quite dark we moved out and marched in double file flanked one either side by men on horseback leading other horses at a distance of a couple of hundred metres or so, from us. Never was the silence of our movement so complete. But our heartbeats were almost audible. Then - there it was! The Sava, flowing broad and dark under an overcast sky. A thick stand of tall reeds marked the bank on our side. Les and I leading our respective files were guided into these reeds where waited two dinghies with a single oarsman in each. We wasted not a minute and embarked six in each boat. Our oarsmen were sturdy indeed; it turned out that the river at that point flowed along a shallow sandy bed and it was only for a narrow stretch in the middle that a strong current created a significant problem. There the oarsmen had to work hard on their respective right oars to maintain anything like a straight course. The boats grounded in sandy shallows among more reeds on the southern bank and we quickly jumped out and made for dry ground where we were met by more Partisans who led us away. What an Olympic performance on the part of that stalwart pair of rowers to ferry us across. How fit they must have been!

While we were making the crossing, sporadic rifle and machine gun fire in the middle distance informed us that the Partisans were keeping the various German outposts in the vicinity occupied with more pressing affairs than checking up on how the locals were managing with their horses. Whether by accident or design, only some of the horses swam on cue; some bolted off and had to be rounded up again. In civil life my mate, Ken Carson was a farmer; he was also a good rider and horse handler. He quietly eased himself out of the line and somehow joined the farmers in the round up. In the end he finished up swimming a horse across the river towing another on a halter!

But I was among the first across. A team of Partisans were awaiting us and one of them immediately started to lead us away. What to do? I had to remain on the river bank until my entire party was accounted for but it was only proper to evacuate each boat load from the immediate vicinity as it arrived. How to explain this in my minimal Slovene? Fortunately one of the reception party spoke enough German to grasp my meaning. Thus I was able to check the dinghies as they arrived at about twenty minute intervals.

On our side it was very quiet, practically the only sound was that of the farmers from the south. The suspense was agonising. The noises from the other side told us of nothing but chaos - horses milling about whinnying, their handlers whistling and shouting and, with it all, the sound of distant gunfire from both upstream and downstream.

A boat load would arrive - nothing to report except that the departure point on the north bank did not seem to be under immediate threat when that crew embarked. Still the same oarsmen - how could they be so fit! But the night wore on; boatloads continued to arrive and the noises of horsemen, horses and battle gradually subsided. It was something over three hours before the crossing was completed with every member of the party accounted for. Glory be!

The Partisan rearguard quickly led the last of us away but we had to march for well over an hour before we caught up with the main body who were resting in a small woodland. We marched on and first light found us at a sizeable farmstead where we were shortly served a hot meal.

Without Franchek my next worry was communication. We were now in Bela Krajina, the south-eastern region of Slovenia approaching the Croatian border. The most common foreign language spoken there is Italian. I managed to identify the leader of our new escort and, having introduced myself in Slovene said, "English or German please." After a time someone found a young woman who had limited German. Through her I was able to make it clear to our new guide that we must be able to communicate at all times and that we must, therefore, have an interpreter. He understood and told me that he would be leading us only for the next stretch, after which communication would be his successor's problem. Until then the young lady would accompany us. In the meantime I should tell my men to get some sleep but be ready to move at short notice.

This I did but returned quickly and asked how much further we had to march and how much trouble we were likely to have from the Germans. He did not know how much further we had to march because he did not know our exact destination but there were a number of American and English officers in the vicinity; they must have a base somewhere ahead and, as they were located in Slovenia, they could not be more than four or five days' march away. As to the second question: the Germans were no longer the main threat; Bela Krajina was of little strategic interest to them except for the Sava bridges. The principal threat was from the *Ustasha*, Croatia's fascist SS whose attitude to the Partisans was even more bitter than was that of the Germans.

The Partisans in Croatia were now successfully recruiting conscripts from Croatia's territorial army. The particularly offensive aspect of this activity for the Croatian fascists was that these recruits came over to the Partisans completely equipped with uniforms and arms supplied by the Germans. This was tending to diminish the regard in which the *Ustasha* was held by its Nazi patrons. We would certainly be sorry if we ever allowed ourselves to be captured by them!

I recall only isolated incidents from the remaining four days of our march. I believe it was the following night that we reached a farmhouse where I found myself in the living room-kitchen with four RAF officers who had literally "just dropped in" by parachute. Prior to capture I had had no association with Air Force personnel and, therefore, no knowledge of its rank insignia. It turned out that the ranking officer of this quartet was a Squadron Leader, equivalent to Major in the Army.

The atmosphere was totally relaxed as we sat there sipping our host's schnapps. Somehow I managed to assume the same nonchalant air that seemed to be the fashion in these parts - I was in fact as tense as the strings of a well tuned fiddle; I knew that the stress and strain was starting to tell on me. After we had chatted easily for some time about the war situation the Squadron Leader suddenly turned to me and said in German, "I'm told that you speak fluent Viennese German. Is that true?" "Well yes, I have no trouble conversing in German," I replied. "My speech possibly may have a Viennese touch about it. I've largely picked it up from our guards who have mostly been middle aged Viennese of recent times. Why do you ask?"

He turned to his companions and said quite excitedly, "How about that for a bit of luck? Just what we want. Perfect! He even uses Viennese slang." While I was pleased that the Squadron Leader found my grasp of Viennese German so acceptable, I was not sure that I liked the way his remarks were tending so I enquired as to why he found my presence so fortunate. "Well it's like this," he said, "One of our agents in Vienna has dropped out. The last message we had from him was over a week ago. He told us then that a couple of the valves in his transmitter had had it. We know that Fritz has got something big going on in the general area of Vienna. The security on it is tighter than what he had on the flying bombs so we must find out what he's up to. We have the replacement valves with us; we must get them to our man up there." A pause. Yes! A pregnant pause would not be overstating it.

"Interesting, Sir," I replied. "Sounds pretty high security stuff. Why are you telling me?" "Really, old chap," replied the Squadron Leader, "I thought that would be obvious. We'll give you a couple of days orientation and dress you up in civvies, set you up with a passport and all the other necessary bumf and put you on the train to Vienna. With your style of local German you're perfect. You'll get the gear to our chap and we can get the information that's vital for us to finish off the Nazis before they come up with something even cleverer than their V-bombs."

"There's only one thing wrong with your plan Sir." I replied. "For everyone's sake, my own included, I'm not a starter. You can call me any shade of yellow bastard you like but I couldn't do it. My nervous system has had it. The very first passenger control on the train would bring me undone. The SD would torture the information out of me so you'd lose your agent and I would be rubbed out as a spy. This is a picture of my wife. By the time I get home, if I get home we will have been apart for four years. I worked at learning German and planned this exercise because we've been separated long enough. Sorry Sir, I realise how important the mission is to you. Nice meeting you, I wish you complete success but I'm just not your man."

"Fair enough, old boy," he replied. "It was really pretty rough of me to put it on you. You've done a great job as it is; you'll certainly get a gong for it. Naturally I'm disappointed but we'll get by somehow; we always do but that Viennese dialect of yours made it seem the answer for a moment. You could have foxed the local *Gauleiter*."

We chatted on for a while and eventually parted on most cordial terms.

It must have been the next night that we reached a village at about ten o'clock. Dogs were soon barking and it was not long before some of the villagers were out in the street to see what was going on. I was soon button-holed by the reporter for the local newspaper. Yes, this place boasted a printing press and was, by whatever devious means, obtaining sufficient newsprint and copy to issue a news sheet every two or three days. The reporter attempted to communicate with me in English without success; he was equally unsuccessful in German. Fortunately he had with him a young lady who spoke English adequately for the present purpose.

I'm quite sure I will never know the name of the place; there was a decent sized creek running through it crossed by a bridge strong enough to carry the locals' small laden waggons. It was dark but the stars were shining. We chatted as we strolled down what appeared to be the only street. What did I think of the Partisans? Was I married? Did I live in London? Australia - Did I know Uncle Marko Zapodek? There were some empty buildings on the outskirts of the

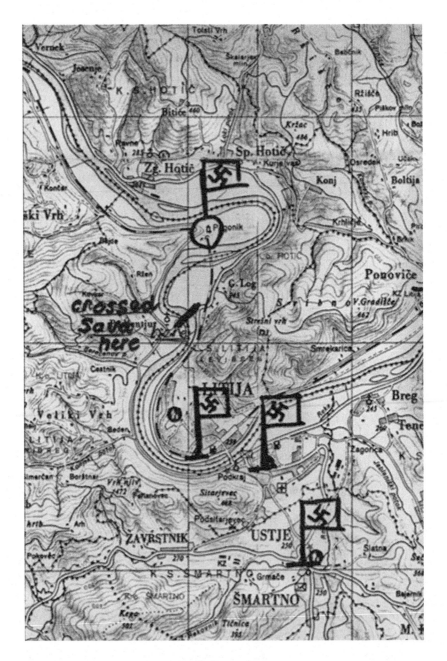

Detail of Sava Crossing

village and in these we were served a hot meal. The reporter with his young lady interpreter in tow moved about among the party garnering copy from an unprecedentedly fertile source. His readers were surely in for some sensational stuff next issue.

We marched on for an hour or so and found ourselves in heavily timbered hill country again. We came upon a large body of Partisans who seemed to be expecting us. But it seemed also that they were waiting for something further. Before I could pursue this an English lieutenant appeared and expressed great pleasure and excitement at our safe arrival. The arrival of any escapees was an event but escapees nigh on a hundred at a time was a totally new experience.

He was here however, to control an air-drop. The moon would be well up in another half hour; the Partisans would light their ring of bonfires to mark out the drop zone; he would use a Verey pistol to verify the Partisans' signal, a necessary precaution as the enemy had managed to capture a previous drop by lighting false beacons. Once the fires were lit we must be careful to keep under good solid trees as clothing and boots were dropped "free fall" to save parachutes. The fires were lit in clearings on the hillsides but it was hoped that most of the cargoes would land on more easily accessible ground in the valley below.

In passing, I noticed that the Lieutenant was speaking with the Partisans in what seemed to be fluent Slovene. Now, as Slovene is spoken by only some two million people as a mother-tongue and thus rarely indeed to be heard spoken by an outsider, I asked him how this came about. He told me that, in mid-1941 he had taken in two Slovene refugees neither of whom had any English. From their conversation he gradually picked up a smattering of their language from which, with the enthusiastic aid of his guests and their

1985

Les Laws (third from right) and the Author (fifth from right) with some of the Partisans who put us across the Sava. The man between Les and me and the one on the extreme right were the two oarsmen who actually did the rowing.

Slovene English dictionary, he progressed to his present fluency. In May 1943 the Great Allies had formally recognised the Partisans and all parties concerned were happy to co-operate when the two Slovene emigres sought to return home and enlist. Our Military Mission to Tito was, at that time, entirely dependant on local talent for interpreters in Slovenia where the Partisans' operations were so significant. Our Lieutenant thus had no trouble securing release from his "tied" occupation and securing a commission to join the Slovene wing of Brigadier Fitzroy Maclean's widely spread team in Jugoslavia. He too was full of admiration for the Partisans: their daring was breath-taking, their opportunism and ability to improvise quickly in tight situations had to be seen to be believed. So far as he was concerned we were already safe behind Allied lines!

The Partisans did, however, tend to exaggerate, particularly when reporting on the results of their operations against the enemy. Headquarters would therefore be surprised and delighted when our party turned up. The Partisans had claimed that they would be delivering ninety one British and eight French troops nett of losses in the early ambush and now, obviously would do so. It was all really incredible. Ninety-nine unarmed men on foot guided through best part of a hundred and fifty miles of heavily occupied enemy territory!

The officer, on a more sombre note, admonished us never to forget the cruel price these civilian freedom fighters paid in casualties for the daring that enabled them to hold down such a significant number of front-line enemy divisions and pull off such impossible operations as they had in our case. The Partisans never left their wounded while ever there was a possibility of their stretcher bearers evacuating them. They never left their dead either if they could help it - given the opportunity, the Germans would lay the bodies out in the local town square as a stern deterrent from further resistance. Neither side took prisoners except for interrogation. Tito had attempted to negotiate with the Germans for recognition as a legitimate combatant but Hitler would have none of it.

Our destination was a village called Semich, a few kilometres from the Croatian border. The Allied Mission there was headed by an American Captain Jim Goodwin; his second-in-command was a British Captain Saggers. Partisan pioneers were busy clearing fields for airstrips wherever a sufficiently large area of level ground was available.

Thus far they had been able to bring in smaller aircraft carrying small but necessary items of cargo or security material where the risk of it falling to the enemy if dropped by parachute was unacceptable. The airstrips, on completion were left camouflaged by day - the German Stukas may have had their day against defended targets but were still very effective against undefended runways. By having several strips prepared or in preparation it was hoped to have, at least one available for a night landing by larger cargo carrying aircraft at any given time.

This would not only make possible the safe delivery of greater supplies of heavier and more sophisticated weaponry as well as precious medical supplies, but also by way of back loading, enable hundreds of badly wounded Partisans to be evacuated to the Allied military hospitals in Italy. Be it said that the Partisans had their own ingeniously hidden field hospitals manned largely by their own surgeons but these were pitifully limited in number and capacity. There were some larger treatment centres where a few British and American surgeons operated with the assistance of local nurses but even these were little more than casualty clearing stations; if large air transports could be flown in the medical staff would have properly equipped institutions to which the really grave casualties could be cleared.

But, according to our informant, it seemed likely that we would be the first evacuees from Semich.

So now we knew. During the whole of the march there had been continuing speculation as to the vehicle by which we would finally leave Jugoslavia. It could only be by sea or by air. Most of the party were of the opinion that the Royal Navy would evacuate us from Adriatic beaches by fast smaller ships - destroyers, frigates or even motor torpedo boats. There was even a school of thought that favoured submarines. For my part I thought that the Germans were still sufficiently strong to deny our people access to the eastern shore of the Adriatic unless the Allies mounted a full scale invasion. If this were not the case why were we still dropping men and materiel into Jugoslavia by parachute?

No! I had always reckoned on finally getting out by air - that is when I ever got to thinking that far ahead. Mostly I was too preoccupied with keeping my party together, getting them fed, seeing they got some rest, getting treatment for the inevitable bruises and blisters, strains and sprains which manifested themselves and, above all doing what I could to create and maintain morale. It was all easier now. Our daytime rest had not been disturbed since we crossed the Sava. I now had the feeling that practically everyone believed we had a better than fifty-fifty chance of making it home early and in good shape. The earlier dissidents were now looking at Les and I more kindly.

But the idea of going up in an aeroplane - that was something else. From memory I would say that only about half a dozen of us had ever travelled in an aircraft. My own experience consisted of two "ten-bob joyrides" in Gypsy Moths at country agricultural shows. I was genuinely unconcerned as to how I was evacuated just so long as whoever was responsible transported me some place where Hitler's writ did not run. Many confessed that they would have preferred a submarine and secretly had considered that as the most likely means of exit. Oddly, submarine was the rumour that circulated *Stalag XVIIIA* Wolfsberg, the institution in which our working party was registered.

It was a sign of the general level of confidence in ultimate success that trepidation at the prospect of the new experience overrode any remaining fears of enemy action between now and ultimate take-off.

The moon had now risen suffusing the steep wooded hills with its soft light. We took cover under sturdy trees as instructed and waited. Many of us nodded off. I must have slept for an hour or more when someone woke me with the word "listen." There it was, the unmistakable sound of powerful aircraft engines approaching from the south. In less than a minute signal fires were marking out a drop zone about a kilometre square.

A minute or so more and it was possible to make out the form of a large two engined plane approaching at little more than hill top height. Two green flares went up in quick succession, a short interval and another green. The plane's door opened and there, silhouetted against its dimly lit interior was the tiny figure of the despatcher pushing out tiny bundles at a furious pace. That mission consisted of six aircraft. (I subsequently learned that they were Dakotas, the armed forces' tireless aerial workhorses, the odd one or two of which, in their civilian guise of DC3s still operate in our outback.) The more sensitive cargo floated down gently on parachutes but enormous bundles of boots and clothing could be heard crashing to earth from various parts of the drop zone.

The whole operation was over in quarter of an hour. The last plane was not out of earshot when a veritable fleet of farm waggons emerged from the woods and, together with a couple of vintage motor lorries, were quickly loaded and driven off to their designated destination.

Chapter Nine
Semich

The Lieutenant had already bidden us goodbye and gone off to supervise the distribution of the "blessings from on high." For us it was once again "Gremo" Our three man escort or rather our escort of a young lady and two men were ready to move. For once I didn't do a head count. My good cobber, Kit Carson, a very sound and ready sleeper slept on. Unaware of this we moved out and reached a large farmstead shortly after sun rise. We were served a copious if somewhat ordinary breakfast of maize porridge , after which we thankfully laid us down on the nearest thing to a yielding surface we could find and slept the sleep of those exhausted not only by physical activity but also by over-excitement.

It must have been well after midday when I awoke. By that time someone had noticed that Carson was missing, a fact confirmed by a quick parade. Kit had definitely been seen asleep under a tree during the air drop and presumably slept on when we marched out in the wee small hours. None of our guides spoke either English or German but I was able to make it understood that one of our party had been left behind at the air drop site and that I wished one of them to go back and fetch him; meantime we would stay where we were. The senior member of the escort was quite adamant: we could stay where we were if we wished but they had to be some-where further along the track in a time span that would not permit such an interruption.

They seemed unconcerned for Kit's safety - he would find his way to the nearest habitation which was almost certain to be friendly. Yes, it was possible that he could be picked up by a hostile patrol but unlikely. As it was they had their orders and would be moving on at dusk. It was clear that there was nothing I could do about it. My growing confidence in our ultimate success still hadn't reached the breezy heights held by our Slovene allies; I could not completely forget that we were still in German occupied territory; even the Partisans accepted that there were still German outposts in the region not to mention the possibility of an encounter with the unspeakable *Ustasha*.

So it was in a sombre frame of mind that I moved out with the rest of the party that evening. Walking away from an old mate in the present situation was a hard decision but a necessary one. I consoled myself that Kit was a resourceful chap and probably better able to look after himself than most. As I record later, my confidence in him was well founded.

Ever since crossing the Sava we had been marching on properly formed roads; if they were not quite classifiable as macadam, they were hard, having been worn down by years of passing traffic to underlying gravel and rock. By far the greater portion of our march to the Sava had been made through forest or across fields - soft going. But now it had not taken the hard surface long to create two painful problems - nails in boots and blisters on feet as holes wore in socks. Appropriate attention to the footwear was always obtainable at the farms where we were fed - or where we found shelter to sleep - boot jacks being standard equipment in such places. Mostly the farmers were also able to provide us with clean rag wherewith to bind up blistered feet. But nothing could alter the fact that most of us were now footsore, weary and unable to maintain our previous marching pace.

However, despite the impatience of our escort, we eventually reached another farm for a short sleep, We awoke in daylight to another group of Partisans and another breakfast of hot vegetable stew and freshly baked coarse bread.

A well-dressed young Partisan spoke to me in Slovene, I gathered that we would march all that day but that, in doing so, we would reach our destination, Semich. It was only the fourteenth day since the raid on the railway but it seemed we had been marching forever. I called the party together and gave them the news which was only wearily received. They were close to the end of their tether and they were getting beyond caring. They just couldn't keep the pace. My sympathy and fellow feeling could not have been more sincere but we had to stay with our guides somehow.

I expressed my sympathy for those in distress but urged them as feelingly as I could to call on their final reserve of physical and mental strength to make this one last leg.

In all sincerity I told them that their march from the railway at Ozhbalt had been truly a very great feat, quite remarkable when one remembered how inadequately clad and generally unprepared for the march most of the party had been. "You're bloody heroes," I concluded, "and you've made history. We've done more than a hundred and fifty miles in fourteen days; we're not going to jib at the last ten are we! I'm buggered too but I'm making it to Semich this afternoon. Please fellahs, this last once, make it there with me."

My plea evoked a generally positive response the general tenor of which was, "We'll be there with you Crow, you slave-driving old bastard; if you can't keep up we might be there before you." Music in my ears. They were still with me and we would do it.

We even managed to put a spring into our collective step as we marched out in the normal single file preferred by the Partisans. For this last stretch we had an escort of five men all wearing recognisable uniform. For some reason they all marched together in front of us instead of scattered down our line with one bringing up the rear as previous escorts had done. Again they were marching at well beyond any pace which we could achieve let alone maintain. I joined them right away and firmly called "*Stoj! Ne tako hitro.*" which was my Slovene rendition of "Stop! Not so fast." I could not understand the reply but they did not seem inclined to comply so I added, "*Mi stirinajst dan gremo, mi ne gremo tako hitro.*" My expostulation that we had been marching for fourteen days and (as near as I could) that we couldn't go so quickly had some effect and our pace dropped to something more nearly manageable. I also managed to persuade one of them to go back to the end of the line and report if anyone fell out. Les and I posted ourselves beside the line from which we would be able to keep an eye out for anyone in trouble.

Almost all the country we had covered since leaving the Sava had been hilly, often steeply so. Like the rest of Slovenia it was a landscape of surpassing beauty with its wooded slopes, its lush fields and pastures and its valleys dotted with quaint peasant cottages. But at this particular juncture we tended to be blind to the beauty about us; a featureless dead flat plain traversed by something kinder to our weary sore feet than the present stony road would have pleased us more.

At the end of an hour or so we had probably covered something over three kilometres. Not far - but far enough for our single file to have become a straggle extending back as much as four hundred metres. Many were limping heavily; apart from sore and blistered feet we were all miraculously free of physical ailment but lack of adequate and balanced rations was now really telling. No reproach on the Partisans - they had given us the best that they had; the problem was that they simply did not have enough food at any given place to feed an extra hundred hungry mouths, I was in as good a shape as anyone but I knew that that final twenty kilometres was going to be quite a test of my resolve and physical strength.

I called for a halt and a ten minute break to allow our party to consolidate and give sore feet a rest. Before we resumed our march I had those whose feet were in the worst shape who had not already done so fashion staffs for themselves from branches of the road-side trees. I then had them march at the head of the column, a measure that irritated our escort but had the effect of keeping the party together. And so we progressed hour after hour in roughly three kilometre stretches - to say bounds would be exquisite exaggeration. Nevertheless I "dips me lid" in retrospect to that bunch, the Frenchmen included. The fittest still managed to walk, others limped or shuffled but, somehow, they made distance without complaint. When I checked with those who seemed most distressed the reply was always a cheerful, "She's right mate" or "We'll get there Chief" or something similar.

Sometime toward mid-afternoon the road wound round the shoulder of a hill and there across the valley, perhaps six kilometres distant was a scatter of buildings - too many for a farmstead - a village. "Semich" said one of our escort. The end of our march was literally in sight. Moses' Israelites surely never gazed on the Promised Land more gladly nor stout Cortez on the Pacific with wilder surmise.

It took us over two hours but we made it. It must have been around five o'clock in the afternoon of Wednesday, thirteenth of September that our grubby, ill-clad company dragged its collective feet down what was probably the main street of the scattered village of Semich under the curious eyes of such local inhabitants as were present. They had become almost impervious to surprise at the goings on in their village following the arrival of the British-American mission but our arrival was obviously something outside their experience.

We came to a halt in front of a modest two-storey house from which emerged a well-dressed Partisan officer. He spoke to our escort briefly and then dismissed them. He spoke fluent English and got off to a bad start with us by voicing some criticism of the length of time it had taken us to cover the distance we had made that day. For a moment I was taken aback, but only for a moment. I was bone weary, stressed and hungry like the rest of the party and in no way prepared to accept any shade of adverse comment on our performance. I literally roared back at him asking how long since he had done a totally unpremeditated two hundred and fifty kilometre march in fourteen days on scratch rations across enemy occupied country. I added the observation that he did not appear to have been missing either regular meals or regular rest; for fourteen days we had had neither.

We exchanged mutual glares whereupon he turned on his heel and disappeared into the building without further comment. Just at that moment a strange looking little motor vehicle drove up. It was a jeep but of course we had never seen one before. The driver jumped out and we saw our first uniformed American soldier. He was a stocky young man and three inverted chevrons on the upper half of his sleeves proclaimed his rank of Sergeant. I stepped up to him, he held out his hand and shook mine. "Congratulations," he said, "You made it." "Only just," I replied. "The last couple of days have been a bit too fierce. We really are all in." "You sure as hell look it," was his rejoinder, "but not to worry, you'll be here for a while. A good rest and decent food and you'll be fine. Now follow me and I'll show you where to bunk down".

He led us to a large, rather run-down building a short distance away that had obviously been the local school. Its normal function had obviously been suspended as it was empty except for heaps of straw and stacks of blankets. The Sergeant, who turned out over the next four days to be a genial and willing minder, told us that this was our dormitory and that we were to make ourselves as comfortable as we could with the material provided. "Sure ain't the Waldorf-Astoria but mebbe a mite up on what you've had on your way here. You won't be here long anyway. How long will depend on the availability of Dakotas and the weather here and across the Adriatic. Chow will be on in about three quarters of an hour. Any questions?"

Exhausted though we all were, the floodgates of curiosity burst. Everyone it seemed had an urgent query and was advancing it simultaneously with everyone else. What was a Dakota? How far away was the airfield? How long had the Sergeant been here? How many other Americans were in Semich? What was on for the evening meal? Our new found friend took it all with great good humour and, as the questions subsided, told us something of the war situation, particularly that which immediately concerned us.

It seemed that, although the Germans still maintained strong outposts in this south-eastern province of Slovenia known as Bela Krajina, they were nothing more than that, outposts maintaining a formal occupational presence. The Partisans knew exactly where these outposts were and kept them under surveillance. If, as in our case at the Sava, any of these positions threatened Partisan operations they were attacked, more to interdict intervention in those operations than any firm intent to destroy. It seemed that our Slovene allies had attained a nice level of arrogance whereby they regarded the enemy troops holding these outposts as self-sustaining prisoners of war.

So far as the immediate area of Semich was concerned, it was well guarded by elite Partisan forces and we were safer from physical danger here than anywhere else in Nazi occupied Europe. The greatest threat was from the Croatian Ustasha and elements of the Serbian *Chetniks* who were reported to be retreating north-westward in concert with the German withdrawal from the lower Balkans which was apparently beginning. Serbs and Croats had feuded for a thousand years and the two causes had nothing in common except, for completely different reasons, the objective of destroying the Partisans and anyone associated with them.

As our informant was thus putting us in the picture a soldier in standard British battle dress entered. The sergeant looked around and acknowledged the new-comer with, "Hi there Captain." We all scrambled to our feet as the sergeant announced genially, "This is Captain Saggers, you guys. He's British but we don't hold that against him." The Captain smiled broadly. Formal acknowledg-ment of rank or military formality of any kind for that matter was obviously not observed in this particular theatre of operations.

"Good evening, gentlemen," said the Captain in a very pleasant English voice. "Congratulations on a magnificent achievement. Long distance marching has been out of fashion in our army for more than half a century now and to have covered the distance that you have in the time that you have I'll wager hasn't been done for a long, long time. But to do it through enemy occupied territory on the kind of rations that you've had must be pretty well without precedent in our history. To me it's miraculous. It's certainly something to tell your grandchildren. It's a privilege for me to welcome you here. Please relax, you really are on your way home. But now I believe our cooks are waiting for you and the Sergeant will show you the way. There must be quite a few of you needing some sort of medical treatment; after mess we'll direct you to our RAP where our medical orderlies will attend to you. I'll be seeing you from time to time so 'bye for now."

Our minder had already noticed the crudeness of such eating gear as most of us had - obviously much of it shared. "Say you guys, you can junk all that stuff now. Everything supplied here. We just ask you to do your own washing up and leave the dishes and cutlery right where you picked them up. Let's go." We needed no second bidding. The comments of both Sergeant and Captain had been so reassuring and complimentary that our spirits soared in a manner that activated our weary bodies. I have no idea what food was served us then or later but it was both tasty, ample and nourishing. As we were finishing our meal and washing up we were each issued with a small cardboard carton which we were told contained our breakfast. This turned out to be the standard American "Ration K" first meal of the day. I've long since forgotten the exact contents but it was predictably sufficient and saved the time taken up by a formal mess parade.

Those in such urgent need of treatment that they were prepared to defer sleep to get it were directed to the RAP. Most of us headed straight for the old school house and our own heap of straw. A blanket over us - what bliss! Never, I would imagine, have so many slept so soundly in such basic bedding.

In the morning we were shown the "ablutions block" and invited to clean ourselves up. Semich was not connected to a "mains" water supply; each household had its own well or drew its domestic requirements from the hand pump in the centre of the village. But there were plenty of buckets into which we could pump our own supplies. Plenty of soap and a dozen or so safety razors - I seem to recall that towels for drying ourselves were in short supply but we managed. By midday all of us had had a -thoroughly good scrub-up from head to foot, a marvellous tonic in itself. Furthermore, as the day wore on, we were able section by section, to launder our underwear. For those without uniforms it was no trouble to wash out their shirts and "home made" shorts while they were about it.

The weather had been generally very kind to us and that first day at Semich was no exception. By mess parade that evening we were a very different company of men from the tatterdemalion crew which had staggered in the previous afternoon. Our superficial but painful foot problems had been professionally treated and our footwear properly attended to. Apart from these chores there was nothing for us to do but relax and rest.

Our Sergeant minder was with us almost constantly. We were free to roam about the little village but were ordered always to remain within call because, with Partisan operations, circumstances could change dramatically and suddenly. Captain Saggers had a long talk with Les and me and took down notes concerning our escape from the railway to Lovrenc and our return the next day. Our going back after having successfully escaped seemed to him to be incredibly altruistic. To him, we had taken sufficiently long odds in getting away with the original seven. While still shaking his head he again pronounced it "a jolly good show" and expressed his pleasure in being given what he considered a minor part to play.

I must interrupt the narrative here and deal with the eight Frenchmen who had so inadvertently and reluctantly joined the party at our first halting place following the raid on the railway. Les

Laws' French was much better than mine and we agreed, as soon as we became aware that they were going to be included in our party, that he would be responsible for dealing with them. As reported earlier they wanted no part of our escapade and made no secret of it. Les established that they were working on parole - they had been free to a reasonable extent, to live in their camp as ordinary civilians working on local farms. They probably had girl-friends; they would certainly have had the best food available - certainly better than that provided by the official Nazi ration scale.

They were certain that we would all be recaptured and that they would be heavily punished for having broken their parole. Thus, for the first few days, they were openly sullen, mulish and a damned nuisance to both us and our Partisan escort. They had been prisoners for longer than we had and spoke sufficient German to communicate with Franchek had they had a mind to but they were not so inclined. It took the night ambush that so nearly brought us all undone to bring them to a realisation that it was no Boy Scout path -finding exercise in which they were participating. They lost two of their number that night.

Les gave them the gist of my harangue following that encounter. He told them that it was not our fault that they had been winkled out of their sweet wartime haven. They were being liberated whether they liked it or not and they would be better off if they treated us and our escort as the Allies which we were. It had little effect. They remained as distant as ever but they did stop dragging their feet and protesting at what was being done to them.

I made an effort to establish some sort of relationship with them from time to time with a cheerful, *"Bon jour. Comment ca va aujourd'hui?"* without being able to elicit an intelligible response. After a few more days, Les also gave up but told them that he would be receptive any time they felt they wanted to be part of the company in spirit as well as physically. I made sure, through Franchek, that the Partisans were aware that they were escorting two separate parties at the same time as far as we were concerned. This was still pretty much the state of the game when we arrived in Semich.

Under the more settled and relaxed atmosphere of the village they thawed out to the extent of exchanging greetings but I believe that they still held Les and me responsible for the unwanted intrusion in their lives. I doubt that General de Gaulle found them overly enthusiastic at resuming military service "*pour la Patrie.*"

Of the American Captain Goodwin we saw but little. It seemed that he was fully occupied instructing Partisan detachments in the use of new light weaponry that was being made available. It was obvious too that he sometimes attached himself to Partisan units engaging in active operations. I met him on one of his visits to the base. He turned out to be a tall well-built young man with a prominent moustache. He too expressed great pleasure at our safe arrival at the base but enquired, a little sternly it seemed, as to why we were freezing the Frenchmen out. He was obviously an apostle of Allied harmony. I quickly told him that they were not frozen out; it was just that they refused to be frozen in. If he didn't believe me his best course would be to ask the people concerned himself. Whether he did so I do not know. As Senior Allied Officer in the area he obviously had weightier concerns than some vague unhappiness on the part of eight Frenchmen in the process of being repatriated. He was severely wounded a week later taking part in a successful Partisan attack on the railway bridge across the Sava a couple of kilometres upstream from Litija, the town near our crossing. The attack, supported by the Royal and United States Air Forces, succeeded in damaging it to the extent that the Germans were unable to put any traffic across it until the following February.

Lest anyone gather from any of the foregoing that I am a Francophobe, let me say at once that this is not the case; I am, on the contrary, strongly anti-racist. I firmly believe that nationalism and racism have brought too much devastation and unhappiness upon mankind to be worthy of toleration. The eight Frenchmen with us had had a much less unpleasant captivity than had been our lot; wartime repatriation was not to them the dazzling prospect that it was for us. I could understand their feelings even while being irritated at their attitude.

Two days of relaxing and resting from the rigours of our march were fine but, with nothing to do but stroll around the village or sit about in our dormitory, a degree of boredom set in. As to our departure, our Sergeant minder could tell us nothing. Availability of aircraft, the state of the airstrip and the whims of the weather both here and in Italy were all factors and all three had to jell. It would, of necessity, be a night operation and we would be given very little, if any notice.

But as it happened, that third day, shortly after the light lunch which was part of the Semich routine, he found me lounging in the sun with some of the fellows. He had with him a young man garlanded with a couple of cameras and a shoulder bag of photographic requisites. He introduced the young man to me as an American war correspondent. The cameraman, it appeared had heard of our escape and wanted to interview me. No problem. Having taken down all the "copy" he wanted, he asked me if he could take a picture of the party.

Some of the escapes in Semich awaiting evacuation.

I rounded up as many of our men as I could find at short notice and several pictures were duly taken. I gave the reporter my Adelaide address and asked him to post me a print. For any number of possibly good reasons, I never did receive a picture taken on that occasion directly from the correspondent but on a visit to Slovenia in 1977, I paid a return visit to one Manek Fux, an ex-Partisan who, with two like merry comrades had entertained Ronte and me right royally on our arrival in Slovenia in1972. He lived in the town of Metlika on the border of Croatia a dozen or so miles from Semich and was thus, the first of the former Partisans to welcome me on my first post war visit. He bore Jugoslavia's highest decoration, Hero of the Republic, and was known far and wide both in Slovenia and Croatia. It was during our 1977 visit that he showed me the picture reproduced and asked me if it was my group. I was able to inform him that it most certainly was, whereupon he gave it to me. I was unable to establish how he came by it; it assuredly must be a print taken by the American photographer journalist as I have no recollection of any other camera work having taken place during our stay in Semich.

In the late afternoon the same day that our Sergeant warned us to stand by for possible movement that night. Mess parade that evening was a suspenseful affair, no further information and nobody saying much. Darkness began to fall slowly a couple of hours later. We were told we could bed down when we liked but there was a possibility that we would be awakened in a couple of hours time. I guess most of us dozed off.

I was well and truly asleep and awoke to the Sergeant, torch in hand, shouting, "Stand to! Get ready to move." We were told to leave our blankets and line up outside in three ranks immediately. I grabbed my old slouch hat and haversack containing now only my toilet gear, spare underwear and socks and dashed out. I noticed that the moon was just rising and, by its light and that of our minder's torch we made sure that all were on parade.

"O.K. guys, follow me," called the Sergeant and we moved out. We marched at quite a brisk pace for perhaps half an hour when a halt was called. I had been marching alongside the column somewhat to the rear. I moved forward calling out, "Stand fast men" as I did so I found our leader in conversation with another man in uniform, whether American or British I did not have time to establish. The former looked round to me and said, "Sorry buddy, return to quarters. No go tonight." "Why not? What's up?" was my natural query. "No go. That's all Corporal." said he more formally.

This was not the place to make undue noise so I moved back down the line quietly repeating, "We are returning to barracks. About turn and follow the front." I had to keep moving to be able to ignore the natural questions which followed in my wake. Having regained the rear, now the head of the column, I quietly gave the order to march. No reason for the sudden aborting of our evacuation was ever vouchsafed us.

Now one let down of this kind was plenty for a company of badly stressed men who had "psyched" themselves up for the adventure of their first flight, but when precisely the same thing happened the following night, I had to invoke the help of some of the more senior and steadier fellows to soothe the protesting majority down. I was feeling as frustrated as they were but I explained to them that there were any number of explanations for the aborting of the rescue flights; meanwhile we were as safe and as comfortable as we could expect to be short of being behind our own lines. Eventually, after a great deal of agitated chatter everyone settled down for another night.

So day five passed with time seeming to stand still. Evening mess at last, two hours to darkness, sleep if one could. Moonrise at last. "Stand to! Turn out in column of three." With considerable mumbling and grumbling we set off again with the Sergeant cheerfully leading us off with a, "Better luck this time old buddies." On we marched past our previous point of return; on for perhaps an hour and then we left the road to march across a field of stubble. Very shortly we halted. I again ordered a "stand fast" while I went to the head of the column. The Sergeant, with the front rank, was standing on the edge of ground which, in the moonlight, appeared to have been mown down as near as possible to ground level.

"This is it. We've made it," said the American. "This is the strip; our Partisan friends tell us it's clear and level and a thousand metres long. That's about what a Dakota needs to get down on. The same goes for getting back up again. The breeze is blowing pretty nearly along it so, if the planes can find us everything will be jake. Just march the men across the strip, right wheel along it and keep going until you get to the end of the strip. Captain Saggers will catch up with you there."

We managed the manoeuvre without difficulty and were soon joined by Captain Saggers, some signalmen with radio equipment and some Partisans. The Captain was able to inform us that the six aircraft were already on their way, the weather was right this side of the Adriatic and no enemy intervention was considered likely. The first plane-load would consist mainly of badly wounded Partisans but there would be room for seven of us; the following five aircraft would comfortably handle the rest. We had already drawn lots by sections as to the order of boarding and, by general agreement, the original escapees would be first aboard. As Carson was still missing one of the chaps from the leading section was detailed to join us.

Les and I being among the first evacuees was more than a matter of agreed entitlement; I had the feeling that a hundred "odds and sods," long since detached from their units, landing on a frantically busy military aerodrome in the wee small hours of the morning might well have some trouble finding anyone who wanted to know them.

"Listen," said someone. "Hear it?" Seconds of silence, all ears straining - then there it was - unmistakably the sound of heavy aircraft approaching but still a long way off. I remember worrying briefly as to how our rescuers could locate us - how would they know where to land? Almost on the instant a string of smoky lights began to appear on the far side of the runway; they weren't very bright, in fact they reminded me quite a lot of the "smudge pots" that I had seen burning in vineyards and orchards in frost-prone areas back home in South Australia. In less than a minute the length of the landing ground was marked out by a line of these flickering dim lights widely spaced.

At no great height a large aircraft roared over our heads. No sooner had it roared off into the distance than we saw, in the moonlight, a parachutist flutter to the ground. In no time at all the new arrival and his parachute were off the runway. Neither I nor any of our party were privy to what happened next but either the original plane or its successor was approaching at a low altitude. A red Verey light went up in front of it and its motors were quickly "gunned" and it flew off. The parachutist was obviously with us to act as "airport control tower". He was quickly guided to the up-wind end of the runway where we were standing easy. It was going to be a neat job for him to guide the aircraft down on to the strip as near as possible to our end

By now one of the planes was making its approach; again a red flare went up. Obviously touch down was going to demand a nice degree of precision. The plane made a circuit and another approach. This time the signal was green. The plane came in with its landing lights ablaze, landed and went roaring down the strip away from us.

It was a Dakota and, by our pre-war standards, it was enormous. In the distance we saw it gradually lose speed, turn around and taxi back toward us. It came to within a few metres of us, and cut its engines.

Now began a positively ant-like activity - stores, doubtless of anything and everything needed by guerrillas in a war of constant movement were unloaded from the cavernous interior of that Dakota with amazing speed and skill. No sooner was the unloading done than out of the darkness came stretcher bearers carrying badly wounded Partisans for evacuation. I can't recall exactly but I think there would have been six or seven of these cases. In addition there were a number of walking wounded who made their painful way to the plane on crutches.

While they were boarding we said our goodbyes to Captain Saggers and our American Sergeant minder who had by then rejoined our group. The seven of us quickly climbed the steps into the aircraft and, on the instructions of one of the three-man crew, sat ourselves down on the bare fuselage. The door of the aircraft had scarcely been shut when the engines revved to a deafening scream and the plan turned and roared back along the strip into the wind.

It seemed an age before it lifted but lift it eventually did and rather more suddenly than I had expected. It seemed also to climb quite steeply for so large a machine. but thanks be: we were airborne and climbing. After a time the sound of the plane's two engines dropped to a steadier and less urgent sounding beat and we relaxed. Soon we were joined by the pilot, an English Flight Sergeant. He confirmed, in lurid terms, that our take-off had, indeed, been a "dicey do". According to him the wheels of our aircraft, at that moment not completely retracted, had flipped the tops of the trees lining the river which flowed at no great distance from the runway's end. Typical of flying missions to the Partisans he said - valiant the Partisans might be and great the job they were doing but supplying them by air was not a duty avidly sought by members of the RAF.

The plane droned on. I think I slept. A call came from the flight deck "Landing in quarter of an hour." We could scarcely contain ourselves. Soon we could feel the plane losing height and banking. It levelled out and shortly thereafter - a slight bump. We were again on terra firma racing along an even surface but rapidly losing speed. Shortly we felt the plane turn about and return along the runway and, eventually come to a halt. A crewman opened the door. Without waiting for steps I jumped out and dropped two or three feet on to the tarmac. For the first time in three years and four months I was standing on ground neither actually nor even figuratively under the control of Adolf Hitler's minions.

CHAPTER TEN
ITALY - RETURN TO THE REAL WORLD

I was quickly followed by my six companions. There was quite adequate light on the scene for us to see a number of ambulances standing by with their drivers. A group of medical orderlies closed in on us. "Speak English?" asked one of them. "Yes," I replied, "Some of us are English and we're all British. We're escaped prisoners of war." "Well", said the medic, "we're here to pick up Jugo-Slav wounded. But are you chaps O.K." "You bet," we replied in our elation; "your patients are in the plane waiting for you." Quite properly the medical team turned to their work and quickly but gently set about carrying the wounded Partisans from the aircraft to the ambulances.

Before the last vehicle drove off I asked the driver the time. "Near enough to ar-past-one" he said. So it was now the eighteenth of September, a couple of days short of three weeks since the seven of us had walked away from the railway at Ozhbalt in the Pohorje that sunny August afternoon. To me it seemed much farther back in time than that. But this was no time for pondering. Our air crew were no longer with us; ground staff were busy towing our Dakota off the runway. All being well there would be another plane-load of our chaps arriving within quarter of an hour.

We approached ground staff people, identified ourselves and asked them where we were. "Allied Air Base, Bari." was the reply. Our further query as to where they thought we ought to report elicited the not over-helpful reply, "Wouldn't 'ave a bleedin' clue mate" I looked around. We were standing by a very large hangar but at no great distance beyond it I could make out a number of huts from the window of one of which a dim light was visible. Telling the other five to stay put and convey the same message to the next plane-load should it arrive before we returned, Les and I set out for that light.

We knocked on the door and walked in. We found ourselves in what was clearly an Orderly Room complete with a somewhat sleepy Sergeant seated at the table. We quickly told him our story and asked what he could do about finding accommodation for our party now arriving and expected to arrive before dawn. A hundred evacuees - ninety British and eight French soldiers to be housed, fed and completely re-kitted: this was a matter way above the level of both his competence and responsibility. He went into the next room and returned after some minutes with a Flying Officer who appeared to have been roused from slumber. Our situation was clearly beyond him also; having confirmed his Sergeant's report with us, he picked up the phone and called for instructions from a higher authority.

Naturally we were privy only our end of the conversation and our end consisted mainly of, "Yes, I'm sorry sir." "Yes, I understand sir." "Yes, very well sir" "Yes, right away sir." he hung up, turned to us and asked. "You're all army aren't you?" On receiving our affirmative he picked up the phone again and called up Bari Area Headquarters. We had certainly ruined his night: it took him all of half an hour being switched from one unit to the next before he could find someone with the initiative and authority to deal with us. He was able to tell us that transport would be arriving for us in quarter of an hour and we were to have our party ready to move.

While this was going on Griff Rendell, a Kiwi member of the original seven had joined us with the information that the second and third planes had already landed and that the troops were getting edgy and no wonder. We rejoined them and gave them the news just as plane number four landed with the eight Frenchmen on its passenger list. Naturally everyone was very excited - why wouldn't they be? We were free men again - free from the constraints of captivity and the caprices of an insane dictatorship. We were on our way home with a great story to tell.

Five large army trucks now rolled up with a large and cheerful Sergeant in charge. He told us that our destination was only ten minutes away and not to worry if we were a bit crowded. I don't think anyone of us could have cared less. The last three planes had each carried nineteen passengers so that, with the seven from flight number one, there were sixty four of us to be lifted. Les and Griff agreed to my suggestion that they remain behind to check in the later arrivals, whereupon the rest of us clambered aboard three of the covered transports.

The Sergeant insisted that I sit between the driver and himself in the cabin of the third truck. He already knew that we had escaped from a prison camp in the German hinterland and quickly got round to pumping me for details. He was almost incredulous. He was a regular soldier and claimed that in all his experience he had not heard of anything quite like it - a hundred men out of training marching a hundred and fifty miles in fourteen days over rough country heavily occupied by the enemy with only a small party of lightly armed irregulars to guide us! "Jesus man," I can still hear him saying, "You **mus**t have been keen to get home."

The journey was only a brief one and, on reaching our destination, the Sergeant, assisted by a couple of orderlies, conducted us into clean, well-appointed barracks complete with widely spaced beds and, so far as we were concerned, completely superfluous bedside cupboards. Reveille for us would be 0800 hours, the ablutions block with plenty of hot showers was at the end of the line some fifty yards distant. There would be soap and towels for us. There would be a special mess parade for us at 0900. By the time we had settled in the passengers from plane number five arrived amid much excited chatter. They brought the somewhat dampening news that they had been brought out by plane number six; plane number five had developed an engine fault that needed the attention of a properly trained aircraft mechanic. As no such person was available anywhere within the Semich area the plane had been towed into the nearest stand of trees and camouflaged. So nineteen of our team were still in Semich.

By now it must have been after three o'clock. I undressed and climbed into bed in my under-clothes and dozed off. I had probably caught four hours sleep when I was awakened by the loud call of "Wakey wakey. Rise and shine. It's eight o'clock and time for a wash and brush up before breakfast." It was an English Lance-corporal on orderly duty. He further told us not to worry about shaving, that could wait for a general kit issue later in the day. We had our "wash and brush up." How glorious those showers were. We were lining up for breakfast when I was approached by a Warrant Officer - I guess he was the Unit Sergeant-Major-who informed me that the crew of the remaining Dakota did not consider the engine problem would be difficult to fix. A mechanic would be flown in tonight subject, of course, to weather and it was expected that the remainder of our chaps still in Semich would rejoin us within twenty four hours. I conveyed this information to those of us present; it was reassuring to some extent but we could not help feeling for our cobbers having for, at least, another twenty four hours, to bear the tension from which we were now happily free.

That next twenty four hours passed in a euphoric haze: the eight Frenchmen, now relieved from the stress of possible recapture, appeared to be seeing me and the adventure we had shared in a rosier light. At all events, when a small truck came and picked them up to start them on their way home to *la belle France* they bade Les and me amiable "*adieu et bon chance*" before fading finally from our lives.

During the day we were all given a quick medical check by a battery of M.O.s quickly assembled for the unusual event of having ninety odd men to check who had just come out from over three years behind enemy lines. Indeed they spent more time quizzing us as to any illness we had suffered and the treatment we had received for it than they did on physically examining us. We were all cautioned to take it easy on food, cigarettes and booze - on everything in fact; this was, of course wise counsel - everyone of us was on an all-time high needing all the sanity and self-control he could muster.

We were issued with a regulation outfit of new clothing, toilet kit, messing gear - everything in fact except weapons, concerning which deficiency none of us was unhappy. Soon, shaven, hair trimmed and turned out in our new battle dress uniforms we were feeling and looking the best we had in the last three and a quarter years. I retained my poor old slouch hat, that, together with my haversack, a photo wallet containing pictures of my wife and my parents, a small New Testament passed on to me by my brother-in law, Jack Bowden, who had carried it through his service in the 9th Light Horse in World War I, and my pay-book had been with me all the way from home. I decided to hang on to it until a replacement was available.

Later we were paraded before the Camp Commandant, a half-Colonel, who congratulated us, bade us welcome but warned us not to talk to anyone about our escape as it could endanger the lives of both the Slovene Partisans who had guided us and members of our missions to them. The warning was a little late as we had already told a number of the troops who had attended us quite a bit about the enterprise. Apart from that I was fairly sure that the Germans would be fully aware of what had happened and, broadly speaking, how it had happened but, in the midst of their withdrawal from the lower Balkans now clearly in progress, found it impossible to deploy the necessary resources to prevent it happening, particularly once our party was across the Sava.

Following this we were issued with cable-telegraph forms with which we could send a message of just three words which would reach home within twenty four hours. Mine to the girl-of-my-dreams read, "ESCAPED SAFE WELL". In addition to this, we were issued with a small sheet of paper called an airgraph. We were told to block print a message in large clear letters on the form for an expanded message to our next of kin; this message would reach its destination far quicker than any letter we could write. Ronte received it six or seven days later which, while on the slowish side by today's standards, was a big improvement on the six to eight weeks my brief pro forma letters from the prison camps took.

It was a full day and by the time we had taken our evening meal we were ready for bed. Before turning in I made a point of asking the orderly Sergeant to wake me as soon as our "rear guard" arrived from Semich. I slept the sleep of pure relaxation. I was awakened by the Sergeant who told me it was half past twelve and that a truck had just left for the airfield to pick up the remainder of our party who had just arrived. I got up and quickly pulled on some clothing. I didn't have long to wait. Shortly the covered truck arrived and out piled our final nineteen, the additional twenty four hours stress apparently cancelled in the relief of at last being safely behind their own lines again.

After a quick word of welcome I told them that their worries were over, they would sleep well and that we would catch up at morning mess parade. With that, the duty orderly Sergeant led them to their quarters. I went back to my bed a relieved and happy man. The crazy scheme I had put to the Partisan commander in Lovrenc less than three weeks previously had succeeded in liberating ninety eight Allied soldiers from enemy prison camps. While regretting the assumed recapture of the six early in our march and retaining a natural concern for my mate, Ken Carson, I nevertheless must admit to feeling a glow of satisfaction and a sense of heavy responsibility discharged.

An obligation discharged is one thing; complete satisfaction was something else and my joy in having attained my freedom would certainly be marred until my old buddy, Kit Carson turned up.

Next day the whole ninety of us were loaded on covered trucks and sent north to Foggia where the Kiwis were taken over by their own people. Our comrades from the U.K. were billeted with theirs. We sons of Oz having no military representation in Italy, were generously taken in by the New Zealanders and, thus, remained with our Kiwi cobbers. Although few of us retained paybooks, we were all paid a lot of lira - thousands, I seem to recall - at any rate it was twenty pounds sterling worth - on simply giving our name and number, our unit (2nd A.I.F. in my case) and signing an acquittance form. We were warned to be careful with it, firstly because there were plenty of con-men around just waiting for suckers and, secondly, it was unlikely that we would receive another pay in Italy. How long before we moved on? Who could say? Just relax and enjoy your freedom within the bounds of commonsense.

We were then issued with leave passes until ten o'clock that night. I have only the haziest recollection of Foggia. I remember that it was full of American and U.K. soldiers. Motorised traffic consisted almost entirely of military staff cars, jeeps and covered trucks with a few horse drawn gharries comprising the only civilian touch. One truck, I recall, had its covering rolled down because of the warm weather. In it were, perhaps, twenty German prisoners of war guarded by a Tommy Lance-corporal with a machine pistol. They looked stunned, apprehensive; they were obviously not long captured; I could feel for them.

The truck was stationary so I told the Lance-jack that I had just escaped from a German camp; could I throw his charges a packet of fags? On his assent I tossed an open packet of "Capstans" into the truck calling out in German, "You chaps are lucky. You will survive the war which is more than a lot of your comrades will. Have a smoke and relax!" I was with Rendell, McKenzie and Tapping, my three original Kiwi barrack mates at the time. Really there didn't seem much to see or do; there was certainly nothing we considered worthwhile buying.

It would have been on our fifth day in Foggia that all of the party were formally debriefed. Firstly we were given printed questionnaires to complete. The information sought concerned the circumstances of capture, events subsequent to capture, general conditions of internment, type of work to which we had been put, illnesses suffered etc. After handing this in we were interrogated in groups of five or six concerning any particular points that our answers to the questionnaire may have raised.

We were back in camp by four o'clock. There was a message for me that I would be picked up by a staff car at ten o'clock next morning. We all took to our bunks, read the English language newspaper and, in my case, dozed off. Six o'clock mess parade - a splendid meal taken in a civilised fashion. We were naturally objects of some interest to our new mess-mates. We were pressed to join a group for "a few beers" in the canteen later in the evening.

I was not late going to bed. I still had Kit on my mind and I wanted to have a clear and rested brain for whatever business the calling staff car represented.

Reveille, shave, wash and dress, then morning mess parade. It was soon ten o'clock and shortly thereafter the staff car arrived. I had a fellow passenger - Les Laws. It was a most pleasant surprise. We quickly agreed that we were in for a more intensive de-briefing than the rather routine one we had undergone the previous day. It was about a five minute drive. We drove into the grounds of a two storey mansion and stopped before the portico. The driver ushered us in to a reception area manned as I recall, mainly by smartly uniformed young ladies all of higher rank than Les or I. The driver announced us to one of them who bade us take a seat.

Shortly we were ushered into an office, seated at a desk in which was a Colonel. We stood to attention while the young lady announced us. The Colonel invited us to stand easy and take a seat. To look at, he was rather "the very model of a modern Major-General" than a 1944 model British Colonel: He had a round florid face, a clipped white moustache covered the whole of his top lip but his pate was bare. His every utterance was prefaced by an "Hroomph." However he was quite cordial and asked us to give him our account of the escape. The young lady with a Sergeant's stripes on her sleeves seated herself at the end of the desk with a short-hand note-book at the ready. He asked Les to start but invited me to interrupt at any time my account was at variance. After a while he invited me to take over.

Escape route

It did not take us very long to tell, in broad outline, the story of our experiences from Ozhbalt to Semich. He questioned us as to our opinion of the Partisans and seemed rather less than charmed with our, naturally, eulogistic appraisal. He opined that they were really only a militia, not to be confused with proper soldiers. I pointed out that whatever one liked to call them, they were holding down a significant number of German divisions and creating difficulties along Kesselring's main line of communication. We were able to state confidently that the Partisans were held in high esteem by every member of the Allied mission to them that we had met. The severe casualties that they had taken and continued to take surely deserved our admiration.

The Colonel then led us to a large scale map of Slovenia and southern Austria hanging on a wall. "Here are all the working camps of British P.O.W. in the Maribor area. If your Partisans are so daring and so resourceful why haven't they liberated all our chaps in these camps?" he asked. I pointed out that we were able to make our break and go to the Partisans rather than have them come to us because of the sequestered situation of our work place as against that of our camp. It was that same sequestration that had enabled the Partisans to raid the work place so successfully. Maribor and its environs were too closely guarded by SS, SD, Abwehr and Gestapo for any such attack and get-away to succeed there.

The Colonel still appeared to be unconvinced. He took another tack: "Well," he said, "You made it in good shape. It's only a hundred miles or so as the crow flies. Why aren't more of our chaps doing it"? This was too much for me. "Maybe it's because they're not bloody crows, sir," was my answer. He gave me a sharp look and then said, "Hroomph! Yes, you're the Australian aren't you." Les put in, "We couldn't possibly have made it without the Partisans, sir, but we still had to do it on foot - at least a hundred and fifty miles of rough going. The Partisans are entitled to a lot of credit but our chaps are surely entitled to some too."

That seemed to end the interview. We stood to attention again, the Colonel nodded to us. The Sergeant stenographer smiling broadly, showed us out. Our staff car was waiting for us and we were returned to our barracks.

I think it was the following day that Carson eventually turned up. What a story he had to tell! He had slept on in the trees abutting the air-drop area until dawn. Naturally it had taken him some time to gather his thoughts and work out what had happened. He had then simply walked down the hillside until he came to road. He had walked along this in an easterly direction for only a short distance when he came to a cottage about which people were already astir. He called in and, though no linguist, identified himself as "*Englander*" and "Partisan". The people there seemed friendly and gave him something to eat. Their only language however was Slovene of which Kit knew not one word. It seemed, over the next four or five days, that he was passed around the neighbourhood from one peasant farmer to another. There seemed to be a lot of movement back in the direction from which we had come[10] but finally someone somehow established the proper destination for a wandering "*Angliski*". Kit made it into Semich by horse and buggy four days after the departure of the last plane load of the main party.

This was the final happy ending to the exercise and I was content. Sure we still had to make it home; in fact that part of our odyssey was to take us almost another two months.

Carson's safe arrival was really the final episode of the escape exercise. We had started out a party of one hundred and five and ninety nine of us had successfully completed the journey. While regretting the loss of the six on day five I was content to accept that we had done well and I was happy.

There was just one thing: how would the official record read? It seemed to me that Les and I had not made any sort of favourable impression on the Colonel who had debriefed us the previous day. I considered that the fourteen day march was worthy of better recognition for the entire party than "it's only a hundred miles as the crow flies". With this on my mind I found my way back to the offices where Les and I had been debriefed and asked the young lady Sergeant if she could secure me an interview with a senior officer other than the gentleman I had seen the day before. I recall having to wait quite some time but eventually I was shown into an office and presented to a quite youngish man also wearing the red tabs and epaulette insignia of a full Colonel. He acknowledged my salute and bade me be seated.

He had obviously been informed of my identity and likely agenda and asked what he could do for me. I gave him a brief account of our march and expressed my concern at the casual nature of the reaction it had produced the day before. Surely our exploit was worthy of more note than a bald record that the ration strengths of this camp and that had been increased by the marching in of ninety nine miscellaneous troops.

The young Colonel smiled at me and asked what sort of recognition did I have in mind. I replied that Laws had, in my opinion, gone well beyond the call of duty in his persistent attempts to establish contact with the Partisans and that our return to the railway work-site the morning after our initial escape had not been without considerable danger. But over and above that was the endurance displayed by the entire party in completing the march, ill-clad, under-nourished and unprepared either mentally or physically for the unavoidable "alarums and excursions" of a one hundred and fifty mile hike over broken country occupied by the enemy.

"Yes, I can see what you mean, Corporal. You have every right to be proud of your fellows. You have all done very well indeed," said the Colonel. He then summoned the young Sergeant stenographer and had her take down a full account of my story. He continued to chat with me in a friendly fashion while my statement was being typed up. On its completion he asked me to read it through carefully and correct or add anything I thought necessary. When I expressed myself as satisfied I signed it at his request.

He then thanked me for taking the trouble to call, again congratulated me on "a jolly good show" and wished me a safe return home.

From Foggia my recall of dates and places is rather hazy but I remember us twelve Australians being billeted with some South Africans. While accepting that those of them with whom we came in contact were probably quite decent blokes, I found myself becoming irritated at their habit, despite having English as fluent as our own, of breaking off in mid-conversation to make an aside to their fellows in Afrikaans. This camp was, I believe, on the outskirts of Naples. It was in that city that I saw grand opera performed for the first time; the piece was "Rigoletto" performed by the San Carlo Opera Company. I remember being most favourably impressed and it is still in the top bracket of my operatic favourites.

It was a Sunday afternoon, I recall, that Kit and I set out on the southbound road to hitch a ride to Pompeii. We had not gone far when a jeep with two American soldiers aboard pulled up alongside us. We didn't know much about American badges of rank - they were just friendly Yankee soldiers to us. The driver called out, "Say, where yuh ahl headin'"? On being told, he invited us to climb aboard which we did saying the while, "Gee thanks Yank, mighty kind of you." Observing my battered slouch hat the driver said, "Say, yuh ahl mus' be Awstralians. Didn't know thay were 'ny Awstralians over this sahd." We explained. Our driver then told us that he had been in Australia the previous year and had enjoyed himself immensely. He was surprised and delighted with Sydney. I recall him telling us that the steaks served him there were "big enough to put a saddle and bridle on".

We duly reached Pompeii and climbed out of the jeep. I turned to the driver, a captain as it turned out, and said "Thanks for the lift Yank, most kind of you." "Mah pleasure," he replied "but thayr's jes' one thing Ah'd lahk yuh to know. Ah come from Atlanta, Georgia and in those parts we still doan' appreciate bein' called 'Yank'." How embarrassing! How could a young Australian know that, eighty years on, the Mason Dixon line still existed, at least in one southern mind?

I remember finding the ruined city well worth a visit. The archaeologists had certainly done a remarkable job of digging and restoring in the two hundred years following its re-discovery.

Days went by - how many I can no longer recall but at last came the day. We were ordered to stand by after breakfast for immediate onward movement, and shortly thereafter we twelve Australians clambered aboard an army three-tonner and were soon rolling along in a southerly direction across a countryside which could easily have been mistaken for South Australia in April.

I recall that the journey was a fairly bumpy one; sealed roads were not common-place in southern Italy at that time. Nevertheless our driver must have made good time as we were in the port city of Taranto in Italy's instep by mid afternoon. The Mediterranean does not shelve steeply there and ocean-going ships tie up at the end of a very long jetty. We pulled up at a large shed near its shore end. Waiting for us here were our Pommy, Scotty, Taffy and Kiwi mates. We were served a welcome cup of tea along with some cake and over this we were able to have a catch up natter. Some of us Anzacs and Brits had been together since March 1942. Poignant was not quite adequate to describe our feelings as we realised that in an hour or so we would be saying what would probably be a final farewell.

In the distance, at the end of the jetty we could see two ships. We were informed that the one on the right hand side was sailing for Britain and the one on the left for Alexandria.

Our twenty one strong Anzac group had now been re-inforced by a party of Anzacs who were being repatriated from Switzerland whither they had managed to escape from captivity following Italy's capitulation a year or so earlier. The leader of this "second echelon" was a Captain Hesslop, a New Zealander with whom I had had a couple of conversations during our sojourn with the Kiwis at Foggia. An escapee via Switzerland himself, he was given general charge of us while we were in camp there. He had obviously heard something of our escapade from the New Zealanders in our party and seemed just naturally interested in the details of an unusual military venture.

It was over thirty years later that I learned that it was on his recommendation that I was awarded the British Empire Medal for "devotion to duty and valuable services rendered as a prisoner of war in Europe" (Australian citation) and June 1985 that, on Les Laws' suggestion I called at the Chancery of British Orders of Knighthood in St.James' Palace, London and discovered that the official citation read "for gallant and distinguished services in the field". It is, quite likely, the only BEM in Australia carrying that particular citation.

But I have digressed. Somehow we found ourselves at the seaward end of the jetty and there, on the left hand side was the good ship "Edinburgh Castle" which, by a long coincidence was the vessel which had carried me from Alexandria across the Mediterranean to Greece in March 1941. Now here she was about to take me back to Alexandria (I hoped) on the next leg of my journey to still far away home.

We were shortly ordered aboard. A few quick handshakes with our "Blighty" bound brothers and we started up the gangway. Despite my happy anticipation of my home-coming there was still a certain heaviness of heart in the knowledge that, among those fellows down there on the jetty, were some of the closest friends I had ever had. Nearing the top of the gangway I turned to give them a final wave. A strong voice called out from among them, "Three cheers for the bloody Crow." The response was decidedly lusty. I doubt that I have ever felt prouder; but I must also admit to feeling more than a little emotional.

CHAPTER ELEVEN
HOME TO LOVE AND BEAUTY

We scarcely had time to settle into our accommodation before our ship cast off and we were away in the gathering dusk. German "subs" were still active in the Mediterranean though probably not in the numbers active there in the four preceding years. Strict observation of the blackout was enjoined on us and we needed no urging. We hadn't made it thus far on our homeward journey to allow any stupidity on our part to bring undone what we had, thus far, so manfully achieved.

I have but little recollection of that passage; it must have been uneventful. It was probably a couple of days later that we disembarked in "Alex" and were straightway entrained for Cairo. Cairo appeared not to have changed since I had last seen it in early 1941. There was an Australian Army presence there and we were able to draw some more money - another twenty pounds sterling's worth of piastres from our pay-books. The merchants were as loudly avid in their hustling if not more so than I recalled. All of us were probably willing dupes. Excepting our time in Italy where there wasn't much to buy anyhow, we had had neither real money to spend nor anything worth while on which to spend it for well over three years.

I recall a group of us being given a splendid tour of some of the less well known features of Cairo by Australia's leading cinematographer, Frank Hurley. I still have a group photograph which he took of us. Also while there I received a message that one Flight Lieutenant P.T. Morton of the RAAF liaison office would like me to call. This was none other than "Bo" Morton, famous Australian Rules footballer (he was a brilliant goalsneak for the Sturt Club). In civilian life he was a fellow staff member of mine with the State

Bank of S.A. I duly called on him in his office and spent a congenial half hour or so with him. I was quite a bit his junior in the Bank's service and he seemed more than a little surprised that I had been sufficiently enterprising to make a successful escape. But he was able to fill me in on the changed scene that I would find back home - rationing and austerity - liquor of any description very scarce, particularly for civilians - American servicemen everywhere. He remembered that Ronte was tall and beautiful and cautiously asked if all was still well between us. On my positive assurance, he commented that I was lucky and that many of our chaps, absent overseas for a shorter period than I, had not been so fortunate.

It could have only been a matter of days, - however few it was too many, I was getting more and more impatient with every delay - and we were at Port Tewfik at the southern end of the Suez Canal boarding the liner turned troopship "Orontes". Another coincidence: Orontes was my wife's second name - Ronte is an abbreviation of it. She had acquired her second name by reason of her mother's eldest brother having gone to World War I aboard the same "Orontes". Sadly, he had died of illness in France.

Soon we were making our way down the Red Sea, then through the Strait of Bab el Mendab and into the Indian Ocean. Although we were told, doubtless to reinforce our respect for the strict blackout that German surface raiders as well as submarines were active in the Indian Ocean, I do not recall feeling any particular anxiety; cloud nine on which I was riding was high in the heavens and getting higher! Nevertheless we were of no mind to do anything that could possibly endanger the completion of our journey home and we observed all safety orders punctiliously.

Our next and last port of call in transit was Bombay, India. I seem to recall that we were there for two or three days. An unusual and warm welcome was extended to us: we were parcelled out in small groups to Indian hosts who obviously belonged to the social and financial "upper crust" of Bombay society. Kit and I with two or three others were entertained by a genial Parsee gentleman who took us on a walking tour of the city with four of his five wives. I have little recollection of the places over which we were shown but I recall our host and his ladies as handsome and charming people beautifully turned out in traditional Indian dress. They all spoke clear and correct English fluently albeit with the accepted Indian enunciation.

My only other clear recollection of Bombay other than that it seemed, superficially at least, to have a more European style than expected, was of a street where women were kept in cages on public view. I seem to recall that they were not actually prisoners but were there for hire - domestic service? prostitution? If I ever knew I have forgotten.

We were probably not more than two days in Bombay but for me, for all of us, it was too long. Six weeks of being treated like privileged convalescents - regular meals of calculated food value, sleeping once more between clean linen sheets, fresh underwear after the daily shower and no duties to perform - we were all becoming increasingly impatient of any delays.

Eventually came the day we were ordered to get our gear together and transfer to another ship further along the quay. This vessel turned out to be the U.S.S. "General Anderson", a Liberty ship. Now, while conceding that Liberty ships were a wartime miracle of American maritime mass-production it must also be stated that they were about as austere a transportation medium as could be conceived. They were constructed entirely of steel; if there was anything but steel in their construction I never discovered it on this, the only specimen of the line with which I had personal experience. Not that I was uncomfortable or unhappy at any time I was aboard her but, coming off a former fashionable cruise ship like the "Orontes" with its wooden decks, wooden doors, panelling etc., one could not fail to be immediately aware of the sheer hardness and austerity of the "General Anderson".

But there was certainly nothing lacking in creature comforts. Our American hosts were a cheerful and good natured crew who soon caught on that they were ferrying home some forty or fifty Australians and New Zealanders who had somehow managed to escape from Axis prison camps. They took every possible opportunity available to talk to us about our experiences while respecting the fact that there was a security blanket over the details of our actual escape. They went out of their way to keep us entertained with movies, magazines, cards, board games and table tennis.

Our course, predictably, seemed to be mainly south-east but sometimes due south. Apart from the fresh air, there was nothing to tempt one out on deck unless one was visually enamoured of an endless seascape of the Indian Ocean reaching unbroken to Antarctica. A week of this, perhaps. The weather was becoming noticeably cooler. Then one morning, up early as usual, I went on deck to find the sun rising dead ahead! We were sailing due east.

The sky was clear and the air warm; we were clearly in southern Australian latitudes, indeed I felt that we must now be parallelling the southern coast of the continent. Was it two or was it three days later? That is now well beyond my recall but I can say, with all certainty that it was a little after six in the morning of the seventeenth of November 1944 that I was up on deck gazing northward with straining eyes when the ship's public address system came alive: "Now hear this, now hear this. The land now visible on the port bow is Cape Otway, Victoria, Awstralia."

A tall American Petty Officer was standing beside me looking at the scene through binoculars. I went completely out of control! I rudely grabbed the glasses from him almost strangling him with the retaining strap. "O.K. Oz, O.K," he chuckled indulgently as he freed the strap from around his neck. I already had the glasses to my eyes.

In the still hazy distance I was able to make out sandhills covered with low scrub and bush. It could be nowhere else but Australia. To alien eyes it may not have been at all attractive, to me it was beautiful - I was in sight of home. Oh Walter Scott! How could you know to write, "Breathes there a man with soul so dead that never to himself has said, 'this is my own my native land.'"

The sturdy "General Anderson" plowed on and soon we were heading north east to enter Port Phillip Bay. Somewhere after two thirty we were tying up at Port Melbourne wharf. We had our belongings assembled on deck ready to disembark; I had an enormous suitcase purchased in Cairo to carry all my "welcome home" purchases as well as a number of non-uniform clothing items in respect of which the canny merchants of both Cairo and Bombay had happily accepted my piastres and rupees. My uniform items were stashed in my "sausage bag" and pack with my haversack taking my toilet gear and mess dishes.

Somehow I managed to hump all this down the short gangway on to the wharf where a number of military covered trucks were awaiting us. I looked at my new wrist watch, proudly picked up after what I considered successful haggling in Cairo. It was exactly three o'clock - four years to the hour as well as the day that I had boarded the good ship "Stratheden" at Outer Harbour, Port Adelaide.

After stepping ashore we were quickly loaded into the waiting trucks and driven off to Army Barracks, Camp Pell I think. Everything for me was now something of a delirium. My brain just couldn't keep up. There was no publicity concerning us then or later. (The first media notice that our escape received was the front page article in the Adelaide "Advertiser" of 1/4/85 mentioned in the preface.)

That night General Sir Thomas Blamey, then C-C of the Australian Army whom I had last seen in Greece over three and a half years before hosted a dinner, of which I still have the menu, to welcome us home. In his short address congratulating us he reaffirmed the importance of our maintaining the strictest silence on the affair. It was the first formal function I had attended since my wedding some four years and five months previously. Quite a number of nice young ladies, charmingly dressed in what seemed to us glamorous gowns, were present to add a softening touch to the occasion. But it was all rather wasted on me; I wanted to get home in a hurry. My longing to see my Ronte increased in direct proportion to the narrowing of the distance separating us.

However there were immediate realities: In the morning the Victorians would be released on leave to their homes and the Kiwis, together with the Queenslanders and New South Welshmen would entrain for Sydney. We South Australians would take the night train to Adelaide next evening. This was to be the final wrench, parting from twenty good friends and true maybe for ever, who could say?

After the dinner we Australians decided that we must turn on a farewell party for our New Zealand mates as well as a "separation" party for ourselves. But we had forgotten that, apart from Melbourne's early closing liquor laws, alcohol was now very tightly rationed, especially beer. On behalf of the party I took the problem to a taxi driver on the rank outside Flinders Street Station. I pressed a pound note into his hand which apparently inspired him. Under his guidance, having engaged every cab on the rank, we were spirited off I know not where to a house where there seemed to be unlimited booze - at a price. How we got back to camp in the wee small hours next morning would probably have puzzled every member of our group. Somehow all of them managed to catch their train on time. I had the good fortune to have the whole day to sleep off the binge - I needed it.

At last an orderly came and told me to be ready to depart the camp in an hour's time. I took a shower and smartened myself up somewhat hoping that I would look better next morning than I did right then and reported to the orderly room well ahead of time with all my luggage. There were several truck loads of us: apart from the few of us from Europe and the Middle East, there were men going on leave from New Guinea and Queensland. We duly entrained at Spencer Street Station and as the train rolled slowly out of the railway yard into Melbourne's suburbia my excitement returned.

The journey seemed endless, darkness fell, the carriages squeaked and rattled as the train clattered along. It seemed to stop for long periods for no particular reason. Some of the others got card games going; others read but I was too keyed up to do either. At last I drifted off into shallow sleep from which I was awakened from time to time by the train stopping and starting. Of course it wasn't purely a military train - it was the standard Melbourne - Adelaide

Express so-called and its passengers were mostly civilian, hence there were stops for joining and leaving the train at bigger centres such as Ballarat as well as refreshment stops.

The sun was well up when we stopped about seven o'clock at Murray Bridge. I took the opportunity to shave and groom myself while my fellow passengers were taking refreshments. My former elation had now become a distinct nervousness. She had been a marvellously loyal correspondent and an ingenious parcel sender over the weary years of separation but was that a matter of love or merely propriety? What would I say to her? These were my worries as the train slowly climbed the eastern slopes of the Mount Lofty Ranges. Mount Lofty Station and down into Adelaide's foothill suburbs. A mile from the Adelaide Station the train stopped at Keswick. This was it! It was here that we military personnel were to alight.

Soon I was in a throng of laughing, weeping, happy wives, mothers and sweethearts welcoming home their returning heroes. It was a joyful scene but, obviously a certain amount of searching was necessary. I placed my luggage carefully in a spot that I would easily be able to identify and pushed my way through the crowd and slowly covered the length of the platform. No luck! I did a return sweep through the by now diminishing throng. I looked about me carefully, even, by now, a little anxiously. Emerging from the crowd once more I espied a tall young lady towards the upper end of the platform. She was very beautiful and elegantly dressed in a light fawn two piece summer costume trimmed with red piping and buttons. She wore a stylish red hat and carried a matching handbag. Well worth looking at but certainly not the sweet, unsophisticated country girl I had left behind. I turned away - then I turned back. She was looking at me uncertainly. I looked hard. Oh dear God no! This gorgeous vision could not possibly be married to the grotty little soldier I felt myself to be at that moment. I walked toward her. She started to smile. "Are you waiting for someone?" I asked. "I was," she replied, "but it really is you, isn't it?" Hesitatingly, gently we embraced. I couldn't crush that beauty and elegance as I had in my dreams.

A pause. What to say? My darling broke the ice. "The Red Cross have set up a buffet over there. Shall we have a cup of tea." We sat down at a table while Red Cross ladies served us tea and scones. I seem to remember both of us sitting there sipping tea trying to think of something to say that would not be utterly banal. At last we got up. I gathered my luggage and Ronte led me to a Red Cross car where a nice lady in Red Cross uniform was awaiting us. She smiled at us warmly opened the boot for my luggage then settled us carefully into the back seat and, just as carefully, drove us home.

ON LEAVE. Private Ralph Churches, of Kilkenny, ...ned with his wife while enjoying second honey-... his repatriation from Italy after his escape ... German prison camp in Austria.

END NOTES

[1] I was the only South Australian in this camp so my fellow Australians promptly labelled me "Crow-Eater" the colloquialism by which South Australians are known to citizens of the other States of the Commonwealth. This was soon shortened to "The Crow"

[2] Styria - Steiermark to the Austrians, Stierska to the Jugoslavs is an ancient dukedom of central Europe. It straddles the present Austro-Jugoslav border, the Austria half being known as Upper Styria and the Jugoslavia- half as Lower Styria. Following the German invasion of- March April 1941, Hitler personally directed that Lower Styria should become part of the Reich and that it should be "totally germanised".

[3] We were paid wages in specially printed "*Lagergeld*" (Camp money). There was very little worth having that was not rationed but when something we wanted was available our camp money could be converted to legitimate currency by arrangement with the Kommandant.

[4] This was the family Zavodnik. During the daytime only the young housewife was at home with her two small children, son Stanko and daughter Mitzi. Les soon became a popular caller, dispensing chocolate to the youngsters and decent toilet soap to their mother. Stanko and Mitzi now live in the town of Ravne further up the Drava valley. I have recently been informed by my young pen-friend, Urosh Zavodnik that his grandparents, August and Elisabeta were evicted from their cottage on the railway near Ozhbalt the day after our escape and were only saved from deportation to Auschwitz by the intervention of a German officer who

had previously been associated with August in his railway work and managed to persuade higher authority that neither the latter nor his family were involved in the break-out.

5 I later established that they belonged to the elite 14th Division which had come so far north to stiffen local resistance. The local Partisans had had a hard time recruiting and campaigning against the more prolific SS forces based at Maribor and Dravograd. They also had to contend with a greater quisling presence.

6 "Good Soldier Sveik" was a famous Austrian-Czech cartoon character in World War I noted for his recurrent misfortunes and determined cheerfulness.

7 About the time in our Greek campaign when retreat was turning into rout, I was informed that I had been promoted Lance-corpo-ral and was issued with two single chevrons. As our situation was growing more critical by the hour, I had more urgent matters on my mind than dealing with these badges of a minor promotion. It was not until my arrival in Maribor, probably three months later that I found them in a pocket of my tunic and put one of them up on that garment and the other on my great coat. When my wife's letters started arriving months later addressed to Private Churches I assumed that record of the promotion never made it out of Greece. I was, in any case, never excited about it but, as my status had, by then, been accepted by both my fellow P.O.W. and the Germans alike, I continued to display the stripe.

8 There was a massive steel railway bridge a couple of kilometres upstream overlooked by an ancient castle which the Germans had fortified. Like every bridge of any note in German occupied terri-

tory it was far too heavily guarded to be considered by our friends as a means for getting us across. It was in any case, a railway bridge unsuitable for pedestrians and impossible for live stock.

[9] Pohorje, the mountains overlooking the Drava valley.

[10] This would have been some of the men and materiel for the Partisans' attack on the railway bridge above Litija in which, with the help of the Royal and U.S. Air Forces, they rendered that facility useless to the Germans for five months.

AUSTRALIANS WHO ESCAPED

QX8000	BROAD, Stanley	2/15 Bn.
VX3549	BULLARD, Lesley C.	2/6 Bn.
VX36694	BUNSTON, William G.	1 Aust Corps Postal
NX9186	CARSON, Kenneth G.	2/4 Bn.
SX5286	CHURCHES, Ralph F.	2/48 Bn.
NX26868	DOUGLAS, John E.	2/4 Bn.
VX29769	FUNSTON, Donald M.	2/32 Bn.
PX10	GOSSNER, Walter	2/15 Bn.
NX1499	MILLS, Alan Hambly	6 Div. Sup. Col.
NX5373	RUBIE, Kenneth B.	2/4 Bn.
VX29281	SHIELDS, Arthur D.	2/8 Bn.
VX6534	WOODS, Arnold E.	2/8 Bn

NEW ZEALANDERS WHO ESCAPED

24990	ANDERSON, L.W.C.	24 Bn.
29086	HOFFMAN, J.	7 A-Tank Regt
29673	HOFFMAN, P.	18 Bn.
33528	LLOYD, A.G.	25 Bn.
15569	McKENZIE, R.C.	26 Bn.
4785	RATCLIFFE, C.J.	19 Bn.
24255	RENDELL, G.M.	24 Bn.
31727	TAPPING, P.G.	25 Bn.
26072	TURANGI, H.	28 Bn.

I regret to write that I have mislaid the nominal roll of the seventy United Kingdom troops who were easily the largest of the three British Commonwealth groups in the escape and apologise to those of them still living and to the descendents of those who have passed on. They were all good men and true. It was my privilege to lead them in the adventure we shared and I remember them with affection and respect.   R.F.C.

In 2017, Seadog Productions, while researching my father's story, were able to trace the son of Jack Saggers who took care of the POWs in Semic and saw them on the Dakotas to Bari. Incredibly, he still had his father's log book with all the details of the escapees. So now my Dad's wish to have a complete list of escaped POWs in this book is fulfilled.   N.C.C

BRITIAINS WHO ESCAPED

181864	AUSTIN, S.F.	R.A.S.C.
2013646	BARRS, R.F.	R.E.
2003566	BETCHER, W.	R.E.
788115	BROOKER, F	R.H.A.
845921	CADDICK, J.	R.A.
830622	CAULFIELD, L.	R.A.
2112047	CHURCH, R.A.	R.E.
2093306	COPESTICK, S.J.	R.E.
2594702	DALE, L. G.	R.C.S.
2332410	DEAN, P.	R.C.S.
2333306	DULT, K. L.	R.C.S.
19142752	EGAN, P.	R.E.
7910104	FERRZNOLO, J.	4th Hussars
1876919	FLOYD, E.A.	R.E.
149442	FRENCH, G.E.	R.A.S.C.
832756	GILLBANKS, E.	R.H.A.
1054772	GREENSLADE, W.	R.A.O.C.
1894608	GRIFFIN, D.	R.E.
902867	GUNN, F.	R.H.A.
936966	HAGGERTY, D.	R.H.A.

1899826	HAMILTON, A.P.	R.E.
1990171	HAGUE, L.	R.E.
	HEALEY,	
111077	HUGHES, H. T	R.A.S.C.
1879228	HURDEN, A.C.H.	R.E.
2068083	HUTCHEON, B.D.	R.E.
1989155	INGLIS, R.	R.E.
1987390	LACY, W.	R.E.
2195975	LAWS, L.A.	R.E.
67908	LLOYD, W.E.G.	R.A.S.C.
1870492	LUCKETT, D.W.	R.E.
2002691	MALTBY, F.	R.E.
2005125	MARSHALL, F.	R.E.
890656	MARTIN, W.	R.H.A.
1605015	MAZINGHAM, F.	R.A.
877182	McNALLY, J.	R.H.A.
898620	MOONEY, J.H.	R.H.A.
1463570	ODDIE, .J	R.A.
2119798	ORANGE, C.J.	R.E.
2344137	PATTINSON, R.	Middlesex Yeomanry
1874271	PENNELLS, R.W.	R.E.
2114485	PERRY, J.	R.E.
1559608	POOL, E.	Northhumberland Hussars
5436591	REED, S.J.	D.C.L.I.
2077642	ROBSON, J.J.	R.E.
908045	ROTHERHAM, H.	R.H.A.
1533418	RUSSELL, F.	R.A.
3604977	SALISBURY, A.	S.A.S.
1989052	SCOON, R.	R.E.
126379	SMITH C.O.	R.A.S.C.
4752024	SWAN, R.	4th Green Howards
558139	THOMPSON, J.	Northhumberland Hussars
937049	THOMSON, J.	R.H.A.
1905696	VALENTINE, A.	R.E.
2331677	VICKERS, C.	R.C.S.
324627	WARWICK, H.W.	Northhumberland Hussars
1568921	WILLIAMS, G	R.A
1557854	WILSON, A.	N.H.R.H.A.
904582	WOLLASTON, R.V.	R.A.

FRENCH WHO ESCAPED

BARRE, Joseph
BAYOL, André
BELIN, Pierre
BUSINELLI, Roland
CHABOUD, Marcel
CONSEIL, Albert
DURIAL, Marcel
ERRE, Marcel
HIRONDELLE, André
KARNE, Etienne
LAFARGUE, Paul
LERETOUR, Jaques
LILLAMAND, Fortuné
MARQUIER, François
PASQUELIN, Jean
ROUGER, Charles
SANZ, Georges
ST AROMAN, Jean
VALEAU, Jean
WAROUX, Adelson

CPSIA information can be obtained
at www.ICGtesting.com
Printed in the USA
BVOW06s2253170917
495139BV00017B/297/P